THE
MinimuM
BOAT

THE
MinimuM
BOAT

SAM LLEWELLYN

Cartoons by Mike Peyton

ADLARD COLES NAUTICAL

Published by Adlard Coles Nautical
an imprint of A & C Black Publishers Ltd
36 Soho Square, London W1D 3QY
www.adlardcoles.com

First edition published 2010

ISBN 978-1-4081-9999-2

A CIP catalogue record for this book is available from the British Library.

This book is produced using paper that is made from wood grown in managed,
sustainable forests. It is natural, renewable and recyclable. The logging
and manufacturing processes conform to the environmental
regulations of the country of origin.

Typeset in Berling by Palimpsest Book Production Limited,
Grangemouth, Stirlingshire
Printed and bound in Spain by GraphyCems

Note: while all reasonable care has been taken in the publication
of this book, the publisher takes no responsibility
for the use of the methods or products described in the book.

CONTENTS

GRACIOUS SEAFARING

DARKNESS VISIBLE

INTRODUCTION

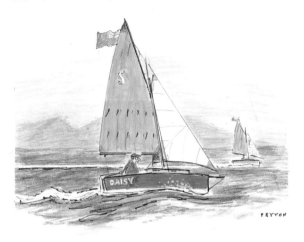

I first saw him at the end of the bar. He was a sunburned geezer, gazing at a pint mug with an inch of beer in the bottom. I watched him half-raise his hand at the barlady. As she started towards him a memory seemed to stir, and he converted the summoning gesture into a scratch of the nose. The barlady fell back. The gaze returned gloomily to the inch of beer.

A clear-cut case, in fact. I made my way across the room. 'Allow me,' I said, 'to buy you a pint. And let us talk about boats.'

'God help me,' he said, burying his face in his hands.

'I am on expenses,' I said. 'For *Practical Boat Owner* magazine.'

He de-handed his face. It looked pretty savage. 'Chandlery ads. RYA Fast Track. Bastards. Gladly,' he said.

I ordered drinks. His name, he said, was Dave. He drank a pint in one. I ordered another. 'I, too, have walked this road,' I said.

He relaxed, if by 'relax' you understand drinking four more pints in quick succession and falling off his stool. 'I love boats,' he said. 'But I hate being at anyone's mercy.'

Out it came.

Your man Dave owned a charming 30ft long-keel sloop, which was down there on the pontoon, nodding slightly to the wake of the lifeboat on its way to render assistance to someone in a Sunseeker.

His house is forty miles from the sea. Twenty years ago, the boat lived on a swinging mooring, and a fisherman friend kept an eye on it for him when he was not around. Then the fish disappeared and the fisherman friend went to work in a factory and the Harbour Commission pulled up half the moorings at the behest of Pontoon Projects, marina developers and waterside apartment promoters. And Dave found himself paying these property sharks three hundred quid a month for what had once cost him three hundred quid a season. His wife did not take to the marina, saying that she spent enough time in supermarket car parks as it was. And the children seemed to be leaving home and didn't want to sail in Mudd Harbour, and it was all very well sailing by yourself (said Dave) but it was nice if there was someone to have a glass of wine with at anchor, and he wanted to go up the West Coast of Scotland but he couldn't really justify all that time off while he got the boat there, plus he wanted crew, and he had sort of got out of the way of persuading people to come with him, and anyway the varnishing needed doing and the stern tube was giving cause for concern, and he needed to work all hours to pay boatyard charges at what, fifty quid an hour?

This was a familiar song. I stopped his mouth with El Stingo, eight per cent, no survivors. The hell-broth performed its anaesthetic magic. I propped the patient in the corner and commenced operations.

'Listen,' I said. 'Once, I was like unto thee. My beautiful 30ft boat sat on a pontoon, consuming sixty hard-earned squids a week. In winter I schlepped through blizzards to do rushed repairs. In summer I sailed in waters once fringed with sandy beaches and now fringed with luxury apartments. All year round I saw too little of my family and too much of my bank manager, whose eye now had the bullying glitter of one contemplating a wholly-owned subsidiary.

One night I was sitting on that exact stool, deciding, like you, that I could not afford the second pint my soul craved. I longed to see the Hebrides, but could not, because of the long and knackering delivery trip. It was at this moment,' I said, 'that a good angel came to me and quoth: "Lo, you have a home with a garage which is empty except for a few geraniums. In this garage is space for free boat storage under your own fatherly eye. Beside it is a well-equipped workshop. Beyond it are tarmac roads, joining you to Scotland, Cornwall, France, Greece, the Baltic and the Skerries of Norway and the Volga if you insist. Five miles away, the Dingestow and Muckross Navigation connects you to an intricate web of inland waterways famous for its public houses. At the terminus of the web are the estuaries of the Thames and the Humber, the Severn and the Dee, from which you may fire yourself into the salt like a bullet from a blunderbuss. All you need is a boat you can tow behind your car, with a decent rig, an engine for calms and canals, and somewhere to sleep. For you are not, unless I am mistaken, called Drake, Knox-Johnson or MacArthur. Your name is Sam," said the angel, "and you want to mess about in boats." And in a blinding flash I saw that the smaller the boat the bigger the fun, which is true, except perhaps where Mirror dinghies are concerned. Under this angelic guidance, I have evolved the concept of the Minimum Boat.'

The patient had now assumed a vertical position, and a strong light gleamed in his eye. 'Hmm,' he said. 'Drink?'

I could see that in his mind the job was as good as done. 'There is of course much to ponder about the Minimum Boat,' I said. 'There is rig, engine, accommodation, luxury or its opposite, wife-friendliness, nature of sanitary facilities if any, and whether it will immediately be stolen by the children. I feel I know you very well by now, dear Ernie –'

'Dave.'

'– Dave, then, and in the weeks to come we shall explore these strange paths together, and perhaps even take to the water.'

'Can't wait,' said Dave, fumbling for a mobile. 'Will you excuse me? I've just got to ring a broker. Boat to sell and all that.'

'Be my guest,' I said. And I jolly well meant it.

Well, Dave became a friend, though he never did manage to sell his boat. And the words of the angel have been somewhat modified over time, for as any Russian oligarch will tell you, one man's minimum is another man's maximum, and vice versa. But the principle holds.

What follows, then, is a collection of thoughts on how to get a bit more out of sailing for a bit less effort. I have constructed them with the help of Dave, various other friends, and of course my elderly Cornish Shrimper *Daisy*. My thanks to all of them.

ESSENTIALS

RIG

Dave and I were in the shed looking at *Daisy*'s sails. Perfectly nice sails, cream in colour, two seasons old. Dave shook his head. 'Old hat,' he said.

'Nearly new,' I said, displeased by this criticism.

'The sails are all right,' said Dave. 'I am referring to the rig.'

'Oh?' I said. 'What's the problem?'

'I have been studying certain equations,' said Dave darkly. 'They suggest to me that the gaff sloop rig like *Daisy*'s is obsolete.' He pulled a grubby sheaf of papers from his coat pocket. 'If you would care to cast your eye over these calculations – '

'Time for a drink,' I said, and he shuddered to a halt, thank goodness, while I poured a couple of jamjarsful from the glue locker. 'Yes, I know,' I said, waving the papers away. 'There is the legendary efficiency of gaff rig off the wind, and the startling performance of Bermudan rig on it. Those wishing to squeeze the extra microknot through the water or nanosecond of closeness to the wind will no doubt consider this deeply. But speed and windward ability are by no means the only criteria in choosing the ideal rig.'

I pushed the bottle towards Dave to forestall the new sheet of equations he was pushing towards me. 'Take the steadying sail. Found on motor yachts like Barry's Baywatch 37 (metres, not feet), this is designed solely to stop the bubblebath sloshing onto the shag pile while on passage. Or the ketch. On some points of sailing the mizzen is a mere airbrake. The great advantage is that the sail area is divided into small lumps, easily handled by singlehanders and those of riper years. The yawl is even better, as the mizzen removes any tendency to weather helm, and in a blow it is possible to jog along using it and the jib only, laughing heartily and consuming fried eggs and wine. In the yawl's popular Drascombe form, the mainsail has no boom, so the inexperienced do not get their skulls fractured. And for modest folk wishing to answer calls of nature, a Drascombe mizzen makes a small but perfect privacy sail.'

'Junk,' said Dave, revisiting the bottle.

'The junk rig is indeed remarkable. One only has to contemplate the astonishing Blondie Hasler to understand the joys of this oceangoing Venetian blind. Hasler sailed a Transatlantic race under junk rig, thinking deeply and tasting fine wines. At the finish line he emerged from the cabin dressed in a cardigan and carpet slippers, considerably more rested than when he had started. But junk rig is not much good for short tacking, an art important to sailors less wedded to 360° of horizon. Drink?'

'Kyou,' said Dave. He sat down, missing the chair by a foot. 'My equations,' he said. 'Where they gone?'

'You have just lit your cigar with them,' I said. 'We have discussed sails on grounds of efficiency and ease of handling. We now come to –'

'The crab claw sail of the South Seas,' said Dave, with difficulty. 'The Lateen.'

'The crab claw sail is undoubtedly efficient, and wind tunnels all over the world bear witness to its astonishing laminar flow, but you will look a prat flying one in the Solent,' I said. 'The Lateen is unquestionably a splendid thing, but virtually untackable, being designed to follow the monsoon all the way round the Indian Ocean, and therefore best regarded by the weekend yachtsman as a mere curiosity. Exotics aside, the next factor in rig choice is cost.'

'Don' talk to me about cost,' said Dave, whose attempts to sell his boat have been unsuccessful, and who has wound up selling his house instead.

'I must,' I said. 'A suit of racing sails for *Daisy* will set me back a small fortune. A fully battened suit of Kevlars for your boat will set you back a big fortune and explode at regular intervals thereafter. The fishermen of the South Seas use a triangle of rick sheet, and get along fine. What is the moral here?'

Answer came there none. I stuffed *Daisy*'s sails into their bags.

Then I put my canoe on the car and selected a large umbrella, for an umbrella makes a fine downwind sail for a canoe. It was time for a sail on the river. When it comes to rigs, it strikes me, we are talking horses for courses. Or so I would have told Dave if he had stayed awake long enough.

ENGINE

I have been making modifications. Out with the inboard, in with the outboard. What follows will explain the sense of rebirth this has brought.

It was a fine day in the harbour, air clean and sparkling and arriving from the SW at Force 3, sea state the merest ripple to clatter on the bow as we purred out into the bay. The outboard, one of Mr Mariner's finest, had started first pull. We glided along secure in the knowledge that our emissions would not trouble even the highly discriminating folk who run the Bodenzee, a cruising ground used as drinking water by several million Austrians. And soon there we were, in the breeze.

I hauled up the main, peaked up the gaff to remove all traces of wrinkle from the sail, pressed the STOP button, uncleated the reefing line, hauled on the jib sheet, adjusted the centreboard, placed the boat in groove 45.5° off the wind, and became aware of a vile stench of diesel. It was coming from a glaucous lane of sea full of toxic little rainbows. The lane led up the wind to an elegant white sloop – the boat, in fact, of my acquaintance Dave. As so often with Dave, the boat was not under command.

So I dropped the sails, pulled the string on the outboard, and purred up alongside him. The white sloop had a *Marie Celeste* sort of air, and at first I feared the worst. Then I heard weird gruntings from the depths, and spotted a pair of inverted rubber boots sticking out of the engine cover. 'Morning, Dave,' I said. 'Trouble?'

'#*&%,' said a voice hollowed by the bilges from which it emanated. '¢∞§¶•ª!' There was a confused hammering. An engine part sailed past my ear and into the sea. The boots vanished and were replaced by Dave's head, distorted with rage and smeared with waste oil. 'Oh,' he said. 'It's you. Know anything about engines?'

'No,' I said. 'Care for a beer?'

Dave made a remark involving bears and woods. 'That engine's no good,' he said, swigging. 'It made these crunching noises. It stopped. It won't start.'

'Inboard diesels,' I sighed, trying to keep the smugness out of my voice and probably not succeeding.

'You've got one.'

'No longer. More beer?'

He grabbed the can with a feverish expression. 'Outboards,' he said, wiping his mouth. 'Nasty unreliable noisy things.'

'You will be thinking of the Ancient British Seagull, 365 pulls to start and an owner's manual that owed its style to the speeches of Mussolini. May I introduce you to the new generation of two-cylinder four-strokes?'

'Spose,' said Dave. 'Start it up, then, and let's hear it.'

'It is already running,' I said.

'Cor,' said Dave. 'But, well, what about charging?'

'On the Minimum Boat we try to avoid electricity wherever possible. But since you ask, ten amp,' I said. 'Deep discharge battery. Optional electric start, but hey, I like the exercise.'

Dave drank deeply and accepted another can. His lips started to frame the word 'reliability'. Then he remembered the pile of scrap crouching under his companionway and held his peace.

'Also,' I said, 'there is servicing.'

'Remora and Hammerhead, marine engineers, do mine. £1,200 they charged last year. Plus parts, course.'

'Course,' I said. 'What I like about outboards is that you can bring the engine right into the workshop. And if you have a real problem, you can post it to the dealer.'

'Post it,' said Dave. 'Rrr. I'm sailing home.'

And sail home he did. Everything went fine until he got into the marina, where they have a ban on entering under anything but power. And nasty little Morrie Leech the sales manager and harbourmaster was jumping up and down on the pontoon screaming, and this distracted Dave, who has a gentle disposition, just as he was dropping the stern line over the mooring cleat so he could stop the boat and warp in to the berth. So the boat did not stop as planned. And I averted my eyes, hearing only a series of shrieks and crunches.

Half an hour later I was waiting at the fuel dock when Dave came down the pontoon dressed up as an inverted sail bag with boots. 'Get me out of here,' he said. 'If I pass the office I'm a gone goose.'

I passed a beer under the rim of the bag. A hand grabbed it. 'We will motor up to the Dun Cow at Staithe,' I said. 'The approach channel has a maximum depth of three feet, and no harbourmaster will be able to follow us there. It is a tricky channel with an inboard,' I said. 'But with an outboard it's a piece of cake.'

SAFETY FIRST

PRYTON

I was climbing onto the boat one evening when I heard a hail from down the quay. 'Oi!' it said.

I looked round, and saw an odd-looking cove wagging a gloved forefinger in my direction. He was wearing a crash helmet, lifejacket with harness, double Gibb hook lifeline, whistle, strobe, built-in EPIRB, GPS, waterwings, survival suit, knee protectors, shin pads, gloves (obviously), and Suregrip rigger's boots. 'Yeah?' I said. 'Let me guess. You are off to the South Pole via both Capes and Tasmania, and you plan to do a little oil exploration and skydiving along the way, and you would like to know whether to turn left or right on leaving the harbour?'

'No. I am assisting with the Rescue Boat for the Under Tens Oppie Race,' he said. 'I am the Club Health and Safety Officer and I cannot let you go to sea like that.'

Well, *Daisy* was nice and tidy, rig and sails perfect, plenty of fuel, all navigational instruments in place, radar reflector up, pumps everywhere, lights working, flares in date. I was wearing a lifejacket/harness combo, some clothes, and a thin coat of Factor 20, the sun being out and the breeze Force 3. But us Minimum Boaters are always ready to learn. I glanced at my watch. 'You have half an hour before the race – '

'Better safe than sorry,' he said.

' – and I would like you to have a look at *Daisy*. I feel there may be issues. Perhaps you could help me brainstorm a way forward with regard to this one.'

The muddy eyes under the helmet brim brightened. This was the kind of bluff, sailorly talk he understood. 'Clearly I welcome an opportunity to input re the safety of your on-water leisure environment,' he said.

'Fine,' I said, ignoring a faint ringing in my ears. 'Hop on.'

He lumbered down the quay steps, slowly, because he kept clipping on and off the handrail as he came. As he stepped into the cockpit he tripped over his lifeline and fell. His crash hat bounced him off a fender and his nose hit the starboard side of the companionway. 'Mayday!' he cried.

I brought him an oily rag from the first aid kit and told him to lie with his head back.

'There are issues re your cockpit environment,' he said. 'I may sue.'

'I am of course insured for three million squids third party,' I said. 'And if my no claims bonus is in danger I will bring countersuit down to you dripping blood on my teak deck. These issues, now. Please explain.'

'Hard decks not bearing sign saying DANGER – HARD,' he said. 'Deep cockpit also inadequately signed. Possible flammability issues with teak decks. Boom unsigned, could give nasty bump to head or stick up nostril. Proximity to sea – cold, wet, moving in several directions at once. Lack of signs saying DANGER – TIPPY. No chainlink fence round edge of boat. Have you conducted a safety audit?'

'I am correctly dressed,' I said. 'My boat is seaworthy, even when some overdressed cretin starts crashing around in my cockpit – '

'Unhelpful,' he said.

'Stop it and drink this,' I said, handing him a glass of rum. 'It is nose medicine.'

Health and Safety drained the glass. 'It is alcohol.' he said. 'Modern studies show – '

'A pox on modern studies,' I said, pouring him a bit more. 'Stone age canoeist or Vendee Globe competitor, we ignore common sense at our peril. Common sense dictates that we take responsibility for our own lives and we do not trust them to foc'sle lawyers like you, and that rum can in certain circumstances oil a gritty soul.'

'I am shorry,' said Health and Safety, bursting into tears. 'Very, very shorry. I had a chaotic childhood and ever since have shown a tendency to overcompensate by bossing people about.'

'You have my sympathy,' I said. 'I suggest you go somewhere else and use your talents where they will be admired, like maybe North Korea, and leave those poor children in their Oppies to have fun.'

'North Korea, eh?' he said, musingly. 'How about Iran?'

'Iran would be perfect,' I said. 'Now it is time for you to go.'

As his boots hit dry land his back seemed to straighten. He turned, an expression of weaselly vindictiveness once again polluting the features below the helmet brim. 'But before I get my plane,' he said, 'it is my duty to inform you that as Club Health and Safety Officer I have to condemn your craft for lack of adequate signage, neglect of Best Practice, absence of Quality Assurance and failure to achieve Safety Management Norms.'

'I fear I am not a member, so naff off,' I said. 'I am however Safety Officer of my Minimum Boat. We have no injury accidents but expect a one hundred per cent mortality rate.' I turned my back on the brute, tightened belt, adjusted braces, and headed for the uncluttered blue horizon.

PERSONAL BUOYANCY

There we were one evening, Dave and Barry who has the Baywatch 37 (metres, not feet) and me, anchored in Foggy Deep, carousing gently in the lee of the cabin, musing on personal buoyancy. All of a sudden we became aware of a roar of wake and a storm of high-pitched cursing. 'Dinghy alert,' said Dave, refilling his glass for the twelfth time.

First there was a rising scream, a splintering crash, and a sound like a Sunderland flying boat making an emergency landing. Then there was silence. 'Dinghy's capsized, hic,' said Dave.

On inspection this proved to be true. A thing like a kayak with wings and a sail area of 40 square metres lay inverted close alongside. Among the debris two U-boat periscopes were rotating slowly. Between the periscopes, bubbles were rising. So I asked Dave to pass the boathook, put a bit of starboard rudder on, edged across the tide and hooked up the nearest periscope. As I had suspected all along, I found myself attached not to a matched pair of unterseebooten but to a single dinghy jockey, floating in the inverted position thanks to the air trapped in his wetsuit bootees.

He could soon breathe well enough to start swearing again, so it seemed there was no real harm done. He was wearing a buoyancy aid, and of course his wetsuit floated as well. The problem seemed to be his Fujito Hullosaila Wrist Chronometer with GPS, Countdown Timer and Beverage Fridge, which weighed about as much as an anvil. Soon he was able to right his flivver and plane off into the blue distance, still swearing. And we reflected a bit more on Personal Buoyancy.

'Well,' said Barry, who was then in mining shares. 'I got these water activated automatic release lifejackets. Course you need to get 'em re-armed every year, twice is better, case of accidents. Pretty cheap really, what, about £500 a go, gold plated is always more reliable than bog standard, my motto.'

Dave and I nodded, each busy with his private thoughts. As a true-blooded English liveaboard, Dave would as soon be seen in a shell-pink tutu as a lifejacket. I myself have mixed feelings. An urgent, striving part of me is in harmony with the Edwardian racing skipper and some-time Liverpool packet captain Bully Samuels. During an early Trans-atlantic race, Captain Samuels is said to have issued members of his crew with lead divers' belts, so that if they fell overboard he would not have to waste time looking for them. Another part, not connected to the first, feels a deep respect for the builders of the Bishop Rock light, who were swathed in barrel-shaped confections of cork. Both these solutions, however, strike me as out of tune with modern safety thinking.

A lighter alternative was modelled on *Daisy* last year by Eric, 16, who had nicked it from under the seat of his BA flight back from a school exchange in Paris. This was a charming object, good for one use only. But it was necessary to point out to Eric that this had been stealing, and never to do it again, unless you were flying Ryanair, in which case they would probably have charged you for it already.

At this moment Dave reached for his glass, overshot, and fell over-board. I flung him the horseshoe lifebelt. He made large and unconvincing sweeps of the arm, as if conducting an orchestra on the bed of the harbour. The horseshoe drifted away. 'Throw something else!' he cried. 'A bottle would do. Oh, help me, do!'

Moved by these pleas, I threw the empty. It eluded his grasp. Begin-ning to panic, I threw the full one. This he grasped with weird dexterity, wrenched out the cork with his teeth and drained a heaped portion. Then he stood up, revealing that the water had been no more than waist deep, walked to the beach and drank the rest. When he had finished, he waved and shouted. I think he meant me to go and fetch him.

Unfortunately this was not possible, for I have adopted a Third Way with regard to personal buoyancy. It seems to me that a boat is going to float for longer than any wardrobe item. So whenever appropriate I wear a stout harness clipped with double Gibb hook to strongpoint or jackstay. And if that means I can't move around the boat to pick up a drunken bum off a beach, well, too bad.

Safety first, I say.

READY FOR SEA

FACILITIES

Barry has got himself a new marina berth. It is very nice and clean and big, obviously, because Barry has a Baywatch 37 (metres, not feet). The marina showers are excellent, being made of marble with gold taps. Everything is exactly as it should be for the man I saw last year filling his bunkers with 4,300 litres of diesel, which gives him a range of 300 miles.

All of us in Mudd have changed our moorings and fitting-out for the greener this year. All except Barry, that is. Barry has what he calls a whole-planet approach, which means that he is going to carry on burning diesel until he runs out of money, which will be roughly when the AA start patrolling the motorways of Britain in RIBs. 'Lovely marina, this,' he says. 'Eight hundred quid per metre per year plus pumpout charges obviously and yard at six hundred quid an hour, plus you get palm trees in the car park.'

'Correct me if I am wrong,' I said, 'but have you just said that you are paying thirty grand a year for a place to tie up?'

'Plus pumpouts and yard fees, like I said. But you answer me this,' said Barry. 'How many times a day does the tide come in, that mudhole where you are?'

'Twice,' I said.

Barry frowned. 'That can't be right,' he said. 'It says in the brochure.

One tide a day is basic. If you want two, you pay a premium for the Gold Star Extra service.'

'Amazing,' I said, because it was. Then I went down the side of his boat and onto *Daisy*. This was partly to get away before he could start bragging about having got the last ever fifty buckets of TBT antifouling cheap. And it was partly because I could see Murray the Hurry, the fastest berthing supremo in the West, approaching with his little book of tickets to soak me for my ten minutes on the A list.

But I got away, and made my way up the creek to Drain Quay, a sophisticated little rendezvous we use for fitting out and antifouling and one thing and another. It is less a boatyard than the back half of a supermarket car park, and it is full of shopping trolleys rather than palm trees. But there is a slipway for getting *Daisy* off the trailer, and Torquil can dry out his Nicholson classic alongside the quay so form 4b of the school where he teaches can touch up his antifouling, and even Dave can get here from time to time.

And as I said, the theme is Green. The place itself is greenish, in a brown sort of way, there being a lot of mud and not much concrete. We are scraping the black bits off our masts with bits of recycled window pane, and doing the fine sanding with bits of used sandpaper from the skip behind a car body shop. We are using varnishes made of copal gum and turpentine, the fragrant sweat of trees, rather than aggressive forms of goo derived from petroleum. After a long and very boring debate, we have agreed that antifouling is all right, but only just. *Daisy* uses a trailer, of course, air being an excellent biocide for most marine organisms. People used to swear by copper, but apparently there is so much copper in Puget sound that the local killer whales are changing sex, and what happens in the Pacific may happen in Mudd Harbour, though it is somewhat smaller and killer whales are by no means plentiful. But we have found some stuff that mimics fish slime, and you see few fish with barnacles; plus it apparently makes your boat five per cent faster, so Torquil is putting on four coats and reckons he will get twenty per cent. Oh, yes, there is plenty of activity at Drain Quay as we ready ourselves for the season in a spirit of make do and mend.

'The trouble with this place,' said Dave, emerging from under his boat at low water, coated fifty-fifty with mud and antifouling, 'is that there aren't any showers.'

'Plenty where Barry is,' said Torquil. And off we went on our bicycles for a marble-and-gold ablution. We all know that as far as facilities go, Drain Quay is pretty much on the Z list. But we have got Barry's showers, and Gold Star Extra Tidal Privileges. So we mustn't grumble, really.

REFIT FEVER

In winter where I live, the mountains are capped white and the sheep are standing in gullies hoping the blizzards won't notice them, and the humans are thinking about the sea.

Actually I had a call from Dave the other day, Dave who has just refinanced his long keel sloop, the one that costs him every penny he possesses and many that he does not. He was in Acme Chandlers, who have the concession at Mudd Marina. 'I am doing a small refit,' he said. 'I am thinking gold-plated winch handles because it says here that they have a dynamic effect on close-hauled sailing and reduce the risk of lightning strike by up to two per cent. I worry about lightning,' said Dave. 'Also I am thinking bioenergetic filters for the pressurised H and C because they may in some cases reduce osmosis proneness. Plus of course I am still trying to sell the boat and the broker says loaded is key. What do you think?'

'You will find this boring, but I will say it anyway,' I said. 'You will have heard the maxim about yachting being the same as shovelling tenners into a hole in the sea. In your case, that should be twenties.'

'Yes. And of course teak decks,' he said, in the voice of one not listening. 'The timber merchant is quoting three and a half grand a cube. That's a great price.'

'And you will pay it,' I said, for it is a known thing that to try and control the whims of a man in a chandlery is to try to stop an avalanche with a wren's feather. Then I put down the phone and carried on with the Minimum Refit.

First, the mast needed scraping and varnishing. I did this with the usual tools, viz bits of broken window for scraping, Epifanes for a deep, bright finish, and a gap year student called Joe for labour. Once it was gleaming on its trestles, it was time for some new shrouds and the odd length of string. I live far inland, so I am spared the danger of actual chandlers' shops. But they are all over the Internet, and very good they are too. So in came the shrouds and the string. And from there it was a short step to mooring warp snubbers. And from snubbers it is the merest inch to the Ideal Gifts section, and Tycho Brahe's Amazing Fungus: Use The Wisdom Of The Ancients To Predict The Weather!! I recoiled with a bonecracking effort. Nobody needs Tycho Brahe, or indeed Joan the Wad. Though of course there is nothing wrong with a St Christopher medal somewhere about the boat . . .

Sorry.

Mast, boom, bowsprit and gaff are now done, rigging ordered. Inspection of the anchor, chain and trailer reveal a certain amount of rust, and the outboard needs a service. It is time for the annual visit to Raymond Edwards, Agricultural Engineer.

The prefix 'Marine' attached to an ordinary product or service usually means that its price is about to be multiplied by five. The prefix 'Agricultural' usually means it is about to be halved. Ray is a small man of razor-sharp mind who has spent his life building and mending machines that must be one hundred per cent reliable in tough spots like quarries and big, stony fields. Ray will rebuild the trailer hubs and reinforce the structure, using lengths of railway line where applicable. He will examine the outboard, express joy and wonder at the jewel-like precision of its machinery, and give it a sensitive and detailed service for a third of the money demanded by the nearest dealer, who is hoity-toity going on arrogant. I load the stuff into my trailer in Ray's cave of a workshop, where rock crushers and the skeletons of vast tractors loom in the half-darkness. I add my anchor and chain and head for the galvanizing works.

The lads in the shed attach the stuff to the travelling crane in an ungainly bunch. The crane carries its load of iron over the swimming pool-sized bath of molten zinc, lowers it in, and pulls it out dripping. Cross your eyes. The shed fades. The horizon speeds away. A white-hot glow fills the sky. This could be . . . *the surface of Mercury*, where iron is soft as mud and little streams of tin trickle through the rocks . . .

Control yourself. Drag the trailer steaming through the rain and unload contents in shed. Inspect covers, awnings and cockpit tent. These have been bleached by the sun, shredded by the wind and nibbled by various mice. De Luxe Yachting Textile Solutions can replace the lot for a paltry six hundred and forty quid ex vat. But down in the village is a firm that specialises in sheep shearing, road transport and wedding marquees. Ted the marquee maker sits among acres of canvas and sheep-sized sewing machines in a wooden-floored loft. He eyes the wrecked covers with the relieved expression of one not being asked to sew up a tent to seat 730 Rotarians, remakes the lot, and apologetically hands me an envelope. The envelope contains a bill for £38. To soften the blow he gives me a cup of tea, which we drink while discussing the fine points of Bedouin tents huddled black under the red dunes of Sinai.

So now we are nearly there, except for some dings and scrapes and a new telescopic whisker pole. The local car body shop does the dings. The whisker pole is made out of aluminium TV aerial shafts supplied by the local aerial erector, who refuses to wear shoes and plays the organ in church. Finally, I make some new locker lids out of best Honduras mahogany. This timber became extinct early in the last century. But in Scotland once I sailed in to Kinloch Hourn Lodge, where the innards of the piano had just succumbed to dry rot. The case was mahogany, so I knocked it apart and shipped it out, and every time I sit on the locker I am there again at anchor, with the mountains rising on the shore and the sea trout making rings all around . . .

Even in winter, the Minimum Boat can take you to some amazing places.

VARNISH

I was down at the yard the other day, and who should I bump into but Torquil. Torquil was wearing khaki shorts and an extra nervous expression. The nervous expression was down to his boat. This was built by Charles Nicholson in the 1920s. It is fifty feet long and every inch is varnished to a high gloss. It is the varnish that accounts for the extra nervousness. Torquil is a Latin teacher somewhere or other. 'Once the pupils would queue up to help,' he says. 'But nowadays it is all health and safety and computer games. I don't suppose you could give a hand?'

Well, a person has to draw the line somewhere, and in my case that is well this side of scraping and applying twelve coats to something slightly bigger than a cricket pitch. So I told him that unfortunately I had a long-standing engagement to put lard on the cat's boil, and would come if I had time when I had finished, and strode away across the yard.

The sun was shining, and people were fitting out. Among the active was my friend Dave. 'Varnishing?' said Dave. 'Mug's game. I use Lorenzo's Oil. Dries to a dark brown gunk, totally bulletproof, easy on, can't get it off. Yes it looks terrible but I hate varnish. When I want to cause trouble in the winter I go to an American website that deals with nothing but varnishing, the losers. I post a message on the forum like why not mix your varnish with Hellmann's Mayonnaise for that easy-on flow and smooth shine, plus you can eat what's left with cold mackerel. Then I go away and make a cup of tea. By the time I'm back at screenside the computer is just about boiling over. You would not believe how rude people are to each other on Internet forums. Particularly about varnishing,' said Dave.

Well, I nodded and smiled. But I have to admit that part of me thinks varnishing is a good thing.

It may be the same part that thinks that my father's ancient Gieves yachting cap is a good thing, too. This is a rare-breed titfer of surpassing ponciness, featuring a glazed peak and a white cover for summer wear. Less poncily, it is made of best flannel about an inch thick, and its parents served on the WWII Murmansk Convoys, so nothing short of U-boat attack can cool the head that wears it. Varnishing is a parallel thing. Certainly the process of scraping off every atom of the stuff, then building up coat on laborious coat, is a long and boring one. But *Daisy* is mostly plastic, and it is only her strakes and her spars that need attention. And when every ten years or so we take them down to bare wood and start building them up again, we are not talking two-pot petrochemical-derived wood protection systems. We are talking old-school stuff full of copal and tung oil, that smells like vintage armagnac. The result, which takes a solid fortnight to achieve at a coat a day, is a mast that looks as if it has recently been dipped in high-grade heather honey, is impervious to the battering of gaffs and the digestive fluids of gulls, and takes ten minutes to patch.

'Yeah, well,' said Dave from his boat, approaching the quay on which I was standing. 'But it has taken you most of the winter to get it like that.'

'Quite,' I said, taking his bow line as he came alongside. 'But your rubbing strake seems to have been less dipped in honey than rubbed with fudge LOOK OUT!'

Too late. Suffering no doubt from a Varnish Complex, Dave had applied excessive rudder and graunched his strake against a barnacle-crusted piling. 'If you varnished, that would be easy to patch,' I said, clicking my tongue.

'But I don't,' snarled Dave, slathering the affected part with Loren-zo's Oil and producing an evil piebald effect.

'Varnishing?' said a voice behind me. Looking round, I saw Torquil. 'So you finished the cat!' he cried. Clasping my arm in a grip that admitted no flight, he led me off to the shed where the mighty Nicholson stood propped among cardboard boxes overflowing with sandpaper and fragments of broken glass. 'Only 210 square yards to go!' he cried. 'Splendid, what?'

'Splendid,' I said feebly, reaching for the first shard. I was reaping the reward of Varnisher's Arrogance, and I knew it served me right.

ANTIFOULING

There we were off Mudd, en route for a beach barbie, balmy evening, broad reach, when I noticed something very unusual was happening. There was a gigantic tower of sail ahead, and we were overhauling it. This was not at all normal. In the general run of things, *Daisy* overhauls only snails, particularly when they have got arthritis. Our astonishment deepened when we saw that the tower of sail belonged to Torquil, in his 50ft Nicholson ocean greyhound. Frowning darkly, we dropped the peak halyard an inch and barberhauled the jib sheet with a tea towel. *Daisy*'s speed leaped from 4.1 knots to 4.15 knots. And past that ocean greyhound we surged.

Torquil was standing at the wheel with the breeze in his shorts, scowling gloomily at form 4b of the school where he teaches Latin, whom he had brought along as usual to act as moveable ballast and deck apes. He shouted something about the Ancient Phoenicians, but I paid no attention, for I was gazing at the mighty fronds of weed trailing from his boat's bottom. Frankly it might as well have been a coral reef.

Later, by the dim light of burning sausages, he confided in me. 'The Ancient Phoenicians used to hang ingots of copper around their legendary trading ships on bits of string, thus preventing the formation of marine growths that would impede their progress,' he said, for he is a classicist. 'So I and form 4b decided to do the same, in the spirit of What the Romans Taught Us.'

'And it hasn't worked,' I said.

'Not very well.' He paused. 'Not at all, actually.'

I nodded sympathetically. After the Phoenician copper craze wore off some time around the birth of Christ, people started to haul their boats up beaches so their crews could scrape or burn off the marine undergrowth on their planking. Then some naval genius had the idea of nailing copper plates to the bottom of ships, and matters improved. There was also tar. (Having once been present at the tarring of a barge bottom, I can give you the recipe for Ancient Anticaulkofoul. Take a 55 gallon drum. Remove top with angle grinder. Half fill with fresh horse muck. Top up with road tar. Place on a moderate heat and leave for two days, stirring from upwind and ensuring it doesn't catch fire, or not too often anyway. One hour before it is ready for application, recollect urgent appointment on distant peninsula and run like hell. NB it doesn't really work.)

From today's hi-tech perspective, the days of tar and copper look innocent and primitive. The bottoms of the world's merchant fleets were until recently coated with tributyl tin, which worked by causing any life form that came near it to mutate, change sex at least once, then die. This kept them beautifully clean. So beautifully, indeed, that studies of British estuaries showed that most marine life was affected, and the muck was banned for use on yachts. After delays starting in the 1960s, from 2009 TBT has been illegal on merchant shipping too.

After TBT, DIY chemical mixtures became widespread. Red pepper had a brief vogue. An American doctor, fed up with high levels of fouling in the Black Sea, antifouled his boat with a blend of household emulsion and 5,000 ground-up tablets of the antibiotic Tetracycline. The boat (he bragged in the yachting press) was clean as a whistle, and very few of the Black Sea's barnacles subsequently suffered from dental abscesses. Or indeed anything else, the antifoulings and other effluents of many nations having done their work, and the water being more or less dead.

So now there is no tin and no antibiotics and the red pepper does not work except on pizzas, and copper (I said consolingly to Torquil) is all the rage again. Torquil drank another bottle of wine and shambled to his bunk muttering incoherently that there was nothing like manual abrasion. So it was no surprise to see his boat up against the scrubbing grid the following day, and Torquil supervising dozens of small children with scrubbing brushes and mutinous expressions. 'I forgot to ask,' said Torquil, coiling his bullwhip and reporting on board *Daisy* for a bonjour rum. 'What kind of antifouling do you use?'

'Anything cheap, once every three years,' I told him. 'But basically, a trailer.'

SPEED AND DISTANCE

PEYTON

Barry has been refitting the Baywatch again. He has bought himself a spanking new integrated suite of stuff with screens. This tells him, among a lot of other things: 1) where he is, 2) where he is heading, 3) how fast he is heading there and 4) when he is likely to get there. In Barry's case, the answers are likely to be 1) in berth A4 of Mudd Premier Prestige Marina, 2) the usual direction, 3) 0 knots and 4) he is there already. This is because recently he has been so busy refitting that he cannot fit in any actual seafaring.

Last time I went on board his boat he pushed a cardboard box full of wires and screens at me. 'All yours,' he said.

'Gee, thanks,' I said, because it was all his old stuff, which was just as good as his new stuff, except not new. And later that day I rowed it out to *Daisy* and arranged it on the cockpit seat. There was a log, a depth sounder, a fishfinder, a wind speed and direction kit, a radar and a gas sniffer, and a fixed GPS that Dave had rejected in favour of one that contained in its bowels not only charts but a street map of Innsbruck. I sat and stared at these things. The first hot surge of enthusiasm wore off. I began to wonder which of them I could do without.

The answer was of course all of them, since at that time *Daisy* had no battery. So I placed the cardboard box in the shed alongside the rest of the junk, and considered the basics.

A log in 1800 was a bit of wood attached to a long bit of string knotted every 47ft 3in. The heaver of the log dropped the bit of wood overboard and allowed the string to run off the reel, counting the knots as they ran through his fingers for 28 seconds measured by a small sandglass. The number of knots that passed between his fingers during the glass was equivalent to the ship's speed through the water in nautical miles per hour.

On *Daisy*, we have tried even more primitive methods. Take a chip of wood and a stopwatch. Proceed to the end of the bowsprit. Simultaneously drop chip and start stopwatch. Rush aft and look over transom. As chip emerges, stop stopwatch. *Daisy*'s LOA is 22ft. If the chip has taken a minute to pass from one end of the boat to the other, she has travelled 22ft in a minute, times 60, makes 1,320 feet in an hour. There are 6,076 feet in a nautical mile. Simple division demonstrates that *Daisy* is sailing at slightly more than 1/5 of a knot. Which is by no means planing speed, but if she is sailing any faster the logger is liable to trip over his feet while sprinting from cranse to transom.

So why (Barry asked, sitting in his pilot house six weeks after his kind gift, when I still had not fitted screen number 1) did I not get a new battery and get on with it? If I had explained the calculations above, he would have laughed scornfully, and quite right too. But I had been thinking. What I am actually interested in, I explained, is not speed through the water, but speed over the ground and VMG. Both of these I can get from my portable GPS.

'Oi,' said Barry. 'Surely you are keeping up your DR plot alongside your GPS plot?'

'Yes, course,' I said. Naturally I lose no opportunity to fix my position. 'I have compass and sextant. I closely scrutinise buoys, tidal atlases, the flying patterns of gulls and the entrails of my breakfast sausage. In a boat like *Daisy*, with a hull speed of 5½ knots, averages are more important than clockwatching. And actually I have got three GPSs, all handheld. So if one goes down, there is always a spare.'

'Hah! GPS!' cried Barry, pouncing. 'But what if the Americans start a war with someone and turn off the signal?'

'I am glad you asked me that question,' I said. 'Obviously, I fall back on my arsenal of compasses, sextants, leadlines and woodchips. And there will soon be something called Galileo, which will be similar to GPS but more accurate and run by European civilians, not the US military. Any further questions?'

'Hmm,' said Barry, eying his screen-packed bulkheads. 'Galileo, eh? Only one, really. Where the hell am I going to put it?'

DEPTH

PEYTON

There we were, *Daisy* and I, close-hauled, surging across Mudd Harbour at five knots by the GPS, centreboard up, water shallow, lead going. Heave ho, and the knot on the leadline said there was a metre under the keel. And suddenly there was a grinding sound and a sensation of sailing uphill and I was flat on my face, and I was forced to conclude that we were aground, all sail set, on a falling tide.

Steps were taken. The engine roared. The centreboard waggled. I got out and pushed. Then I put the anchor rode on the peak halliard and laid it out in the dinghy and heaved until *Daisy* was just about lying on her side. Then I got out and pushed again. Nothing availed. We were stuck as if concreted to the bottom. The only solution was to clamber back aboard, make a cup of tea and try to look as if we were sitting here on purpose, enjoying the light rain that had begun to fall. It was at this point that Barry came alongside in his RIB.

Barry has the deep understanding of human nature you would expect in someone who spent his formative years flogging used Vauxhalls to the unwary. He saw through my little ruse instantly. 'Sounder packed up?' he said.

'Mmf,' I said.

'I got two,' said Barry.

This is true. They sit with the sixty or seventy other little screens on his console, if that is the right word for his jittering migraine of electronics. It was also true that my sounder was faulty. It is the knots that are the problem.

Traditionally, knots have no place on a leadline. According to an 1891 *Text-Book of Seamanship*, markings are as follows: At two fathoms from the lead, two strips of leather. At three fathoms from the lead, three strips of leather. At five fathoms from the lead, a white rag. At seven fathoms from the lead, a red rag. At ten fathoms from the lead, a bit of leather having a hole in it. At thirteen fathoms from the lead, as at three. At fifteen fathoms from the lead, as at five. At seventeen fathoms from the lead, as at seven. There are other marks, but by the time you get to seventeen fathoms you are already wading round the cockpit with thirty metres of line round your ankles, cursing horribly.

The reason for all this cloth and leather is to be recognizable in the dark, and perhaps it works, but not for me. (Bit of leather with a hole in it? Ten fathoms. Or was that thirteen? Soddit soddit oops it's round the propellor oh hell now we're aground.) In a bid for simplicity, I replaced the Christmas decorations with knots: one for one metre, two for two, and so on. But I used thumb knots. And thumb knots have a nasty way of migrating up and down the line they are tied in while you are not looking. The two-metre knots on my line had migrated towards the lead. Hence my predicament on the sandbank, and Barry's smug laughter.

While I waited for the tide I made some resolutions. The next day I resurrected from the shed a Seafarer depth sounder. This fossil has a spinning disc which produces a red glow undimmed since the late 1960s, when it was manufactured. It is calibrated in fathoms, so I cut out a metre scale for it, easily dismountable in the event of *Daisy* ever crossing the Atlantic. The battery connector was configured for 9 volt batteries of ancient design and vast price, and its transducer cable is black as your hat and crumbles at the touch. But a disused home smoke alarm produced a connector that fits a new-style 9 volt battery. A quick blast on eBay produced a new transducer. And a visit to the Plumb Centre produced a quid's worth of 40mm grey pipe that fitted the transducer like ham fits eggs. Singing cheerily, we epoxied the bit of drainpipe to the boat's bilges, filled the tube with a spot of extra virgin olive oil, shoved the transducer home and fired it up. And there was the depth, twinkling away like Mars in a heat haze. And here we are now, negotiating a maze of banks where Barry fears to tread. The disc is whirring, the transducer nestles in the bilges and all's right with the world. Minimum depth? I'll check the sounder.

CRUISING
WHERE THIS YEAR?

The view from the rain-spattered bar window of Mudd
Sailing Club was not an enticing one. The harbour looked like a sheet
of wet slate. A couple of boats tugged fractiously at their moorings.
Inside, the view was better, featuring a table covered with mixed stimulants. Round this table sat Barry, our host, Dave, and me, of course.
All our boats were out of sight, but not out of mind. For we were
discussing our cruising plans for next year.

'Yeah, well,' said Barry, who at this point had something to do with
selling houses, or maybe building them, or perhaps it was mining shares.
'Cruising is all about getting pole position in marinas. I mean what's
the good of spending two whole days getting from the Solent to Puerto
Banus if nobody can see you when you get there? Like when you fire
up a Havana in San Trop you want to be close enough to bleedin' Nicole
Kidman for her to *smell* it. Harbours to visit? Like I said, Puerto Banus
San Trop Monte Carlo at a pinch and Portofino. Maybe the wife will
come along this year.' He scowled. 'Hope not,' he said.

Dave frowned. 'Who is Nicole Kidman?' he said. 'I thought Iceland.
Marvellous place. Hundreds of miles of sea. No trees, of course, but
who needs trees? Land,' says Dave, 'horrid gritty stuff. Hate it really.
Ah, yes. We will beat the whale-road with the dragon-hammer of our
bows. Where are you off to then?' he said, looking at me.

I did not reply immediately, for Dave's plans were making me shiver, rather as if a whale had mistaken my backbone for a road and was taking a stroll up it. 'I dunno,' I said. 'Though I have always fancied circumnavigating Eurasia. Never been done in a Cornish Shrimper as far as I know.'

Dave was already sucking his teeth in a judicious manner. 'The Red Sea is very dodgy at the moment,' he said, like he knew.

'True,' I said consideringly. 'And global warming or no global warming, there's a lot of ice in the Kara Sea.'

'Kara wha?' said Barry, with the narrowed eyes of a lifelong salesman who feels he is missing a trick.

'Up by Novaya Zemlya there,' I said. 'You know. Big island near the Russian missile ranges.'

'Oh, *that* Novaya Zemlya,' said Barry, panicking visibly. 'Anyone want a drink?' And off he hurried to regroup.

Outside the window the grim afternoon was becoming the grim evening. 'Eurasia? In a Shrimper? For real?' said Dave out of the side of his mouth.

'Listen,' I said. 'We know two main things about cruising, and Barry does not know either of them. One is that making plans in January is sometimes a lot more fun than actually carrying out those plans in July, particularly if they involve icebergs. And the other is that cruising is all about moments. It is good to pull up anchor in the morning and go to sea. It is good to make landfall and tie up and swagger ashore even if you have only got to the far side of Mudd Harbour, because even that journey of three miles will give you a small inkling of the emotions experienced by Francis Drake when strolling onto the quay for a spot of larceny on the Spanish Main. Also it is fun to do some fishing and trim some sails and sit in a creek and imbibe a spot of the ruby and talk nonsense and make small but significant alterations to the fabric and amenities of your boat. And to wind up your friends, of course. A dark curse on St Tropez, and the same goes for Iceland and Novaya Zemlya. Oh, look, here comes Barry.'

Barry sat down. He said, 'I've been thinking.'

'Hmm?' we said.

'San Trop is all very well,' he said. 'But I think I could get the air conditioning turned into heating and have a go at the Northwest Passage.'

'Attaboy!' we cried.

'See you there, then?' said Barry.

I gazed out of the window at the wintry horror of Mudd Harbour. By July it would all be blue and warm and lovely, and the stars would be bulging over the creeks, and the churring of the nightjars would be floating over the anchorages.

'Maybe, maybe not,' I said. 'It's a big planet.'

SELL UP AND SAIL

There is always a lot of Boat Show fallout in Mudd Harbour. For weeks you see people staggering around wearing expressions of numb terror. Normally this is because they are wondering how to tell the life's partner that after a few triples in the Wealth Management suite they have inadvertently ordered a Swan 67. But since the crunch things have been different. People are looking not so much haunted as resigned yet lustful, like diabetics in a sweetshop.

Not Dave, though. Nowadays Dave lives aboard the only long-keel sloop with garden shed cockpit and stove pipe in the wide grey wastes of Mudd Harbour. Since the onset of winter, the bits of his face visible between the brim of his woolly hat and the polo neck of his jersey have become pinched and bluish. But at a Boat Show I spotted him talking to a woman with a tan and bridgework, who was sitting under a sign that said The Ocean My Home. And when I bumped into him back in Mudd the woolly garments were in place, but the features had a sort of messianic glow.

'All right,' I said, accompanying him into the Harbour View Bar of the Mermaid. 'So what is it this time?'

Dave gazed out at the steady plunge of the sleet into the lead-coloured water. 'Transoceanic cookery,' he murmured. 'Hurricane management. Lime juice.'

'*What?*'

'I bought a book. I am planning to sell up and sail,' he said.

'Ah.' A bit more sleet fell. 'But you have already sold up, and you live on your boat.'

'That was the bank manager,' said Dave. 'This is Free Will. I'm off. Canaries, West Indies, Brazil, the Capes. Do you realise I have never seen an albatross, let alone a penguin? Everyone wants to. Eh?' He fixed me with a burning eye.

He was right, of course. Every year I fit *Daisy* out with a view to a grand expedition northwards to cruise slowly through places I visited in a hurry in past years. Scotland in detail. Then Norway, round into the Baltic, back up to the North Cape, chance of a narwhal, Northeast passage. And every year there is an excellent reason why it is impossible to go.

Dave sighed. 'But I never got round to doing it,' he said. 'And I probably won't this time. There's always a good reason to stay. What I need is a good reason to go.'

Here Barry entered in his blazer, with the lovely Chantelle on his arm in suntan and white linen, both shouting for champagne. This was odd, for Barry's business was not going very well, what with the economic situation, and Mrs Barry having found out about Chantelle, and the expense of owning a Baywatch 37 (metres, not feet). But champagne is champagne, so down it went, and someone asked Barry about the Boat Show. 'I bought charts,' he said.

'Approaches to the Turks and Caicos Islands,' said Chantelle, and giggled.

'Wait a minute,' said Dave. 'Didn't I see you with the *Ocean My Home* lady?'

'Me? Never,' said Barry, as if shocked, and Chantelle giggled again. Somehow my eye strayed out of the window to the New Harbour, where the fishing boats live. On the outside of the quay was the loom of a big boat. It looked very like Barry's. And the things lashed all over its deck and cockpit looked very like drums of spare fuel.

'Well, ta-ra, then,' said Barry, and the last thing we heard as they headed into the downpour was Chantelle's giggle.

Next morning Dave rang. He said, 'Get down to the New Harbour.'

Down I went. Barry's Baywatch was gone. The quay was swarming with people in dark suits and clipboards. 'HMRC,' said one of them, glaring over his specs. 'These other officers are from the banks, the wine merchants and the chandlers. We are seeking a Mr Barry Barrington, owner of the yacht *Capitalist Tool*. Have you seen him?'

'Not recently,' I said. 'What's he done?'

'A runner,' said the suit. 'VAT. Income tax. Bollinger. Wife. You name it.'

'Dear me,' I said, and I could see Dave saying the same thing at the other end of the quay, innocent as a baby. 'What a terrible thing.'

'A wanted felon,' said the taxman. 'Tchah.'

I gave him a kind smile. 'I prefer to think that he has decided to sell up and sail,' I said. 'And that unlike a lot of us, he has found a very good reason.'

MINIMUM FLOTILLA

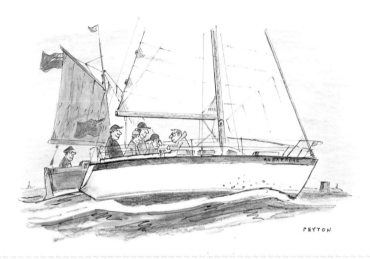

PEYTON

So there I was somewhere off the west of Scotland, filling up *Daisy*'s water jerrycan from the never failing spring behind the quay, when I saw this New Zealand bloke gazing out to sea and muttering tensely into a handheld VHF. 'No, Mr Bockles,' he was saying. 'Turn to port. Left. Not that left, the other left.' Crackle. 'I am sorry your wife is upset because the hair dryer is not working. We will talk about it later. Now on your right you will see Mr Withers. He is about to collide, correction, has already collided with you. I am sorry you do not like the CDs and the tiller is not what you are used to. Oh God damn you all, you lubbers from hell.' Casting the handheld into the sea, he stumped off in the direction of the pub.

At this point I noticed that the horizon was thick with sails. And it all became clear. I was in the presence of a Flotilla, and it was heading for the quay.

There was no time to lose. Heaving the water breaker into *Daisy*'s cockpit, I let go the shore lines and sailed away to the secluded harbour where my friends were waiting in their boats. Adding a spot of whisky to some of the spring water, we chatted for a while. Then I took a dinghy ashore to forage for the odd mussel.

Just round the point, a man in new shorts was sitting on a tuft of sea pinks scowling at a dead shrimp. Below him, a small inflatable was bumping nastily on the rocks. Rendered expansive by the high-quality spring water I asked him what his problem was. He laughed bitterly. 'Flotillas!' he said.

'Flotillas are lovely,' I said, indicating our small raft of identical boats.

'Huh,' he said. I deduced that here was a flotillero who had come here to sulk, and was in need of therapy. Sigmund Freud, father of headshrinking, said that the therapist's job is to listen. I therefore held my peace.

'They squash you into these boats, me and the wife and the wife's sister and her husband,' said the flotillero. 'There is always someone else who wants to be captain.'

'Whereas the captain is rightfully you?' I murmured.

'Obviously. I am easily the most experienced person on board. I have,' he said with quiet pride, 'a Competent Crew (Shore Based) Certificate. But that b----, er, brother-in-law says I smacked the quay in Oban and Dunstaffnage and wrapped up something shocking in Tobermory. Isolated incidents, all of them.' He shook his head. 'Plus the wife and her sister say I shout. I mean how is a captain supposed to make himself heard? Is that whisky?'

'Cold tea,' I said, for stimulants have no place in a therapeutic conversation of this kind, and I felt we were on the verge of a breakthrough.

'Pity,' he said. 'Anyway a Trappist monk would be shouting if he was getting the amount of sleep I am getting. They all snore.'

'Most people do,' I said.

'Not me,' he said. 'Don't get the chance. As soon as I doze off they wake me up. The other night they made me stand anchor watch. In a marina. And me the captain.'

This was obviously an all but hopeless case, and moreover a hopeless case that snored and was in denial. I said, with some asperity, that I had met many delightful and well-adjusted people who valued the camaraderie of flotilla sailing. 'As for us,' I said, indicating our five-boat raft, 'we are a Minimum Flotilla, an arrangement which combines sailing, safety, folk song and – '

'Yeah, fascinating, is that the time already?' said the flotillero, looking at his watch.

'Consider the jellyfish,' I said, getting between him and his tender.

'No,' he said.

'A jellyfish,' I said, 'is a loose group of feeding cells, stinging cells and motivating cells. The Minimum Flotilla is roughly the same thing with singing instead of stinging. Each of the five of us sails our own boat, singlehanded. In the mornings we set off in a loose gaggle for a destination predetermined by discussion of weather forecast, tidal gates and exquisite beauty. Breakfast is taken in peaceful solitude, and the sensitive morning hours pass in solosail handling, helmsmanship, and constant vigilance for the safety and well-being of our comrades. If the occasion presents itself, at lunchtime we anchor and chat of this and that. If not, there is ongoing competition about the number of eggs that can be fried while trucking under full sail without autopilot, extra points being awarded for self-caught mackerel. In the evening we anchor and raft up, the raft being 19ft long and 35ft wide, i.e. pretty big. Communal cookery takes place, wine is drunk and lies are told. After which there is a spot of guitar playing. When a drowsy numbness pains the sense, we all let go fore and aft, separate and lie to our anchors. Some of us are world class snorers,' I said. 'But none of us has ever been kept awake by any of the others snoring.'

The patient was now showing signs of scepticism. 'What about cold beer?' he said. 'And hot water?'

'If you want freezing and boiling, try the Milton Keynes Travelodge,' I said. 'The sea is cool, and solar showers are warmish. Our pleasure is in artful contrivance.'

He gave a thin little laugh and said something about being late for a Group Pub Visit and his wife killing him. Then he was in his dinghy, firing up the outboard and screaming off to nowhere at full throttle. As I drifted back to the boats an otter was champing an eel in the shallows. There was the pop of a cork leaving a bottle. I began to scrub mussels, while my fellow-flotillero Bertie boiled spuds in seawater and Venus rode the moon into the sky.

The Minimum Flotilla evening had begun.

FOOD

There I was, sitting in the anchorage all a-tanto, glass of wine in hand, watching the anchor light on the only other boat wobbling in the water. When suddenly there was a dull explosion and a storm of cursing. And on the other boat's deck there appeared a figure beating at his clothes, which appeared to be smouldering.

He jumped into the water and then remembered that he had no ladder over the side and started hooting in a large dim voice. So I fished him out, helped him extinguish his galley, established that his burns were merely cosmetic, and listened to his story.

'Effing dual fuel cookers,' he said. 'Man at the Boat Show said they were all the rage. I mean how was I to know that you were not meant to squirt the meths onto the paraffin in case it turns out the paraffin was still lit? Bang went the Reddimeal. Bang went the boat, near enough.'

I pursed my lips. Dual fuel is a snare, and Reddimeals have no part to play in the victualling of the Minimum Boat.

On the Minimum Boat, food is simple, nourishing and occasionally edible. The Navy of Patrick O'Brian and C S Forester won its wars on salt horse, ship's biscuit and the odd penguin's egg. Advances in tinning technology mean that there is no longer any need to go around salting horses. Ship's biscuit, however, still has its uses, so here is the recipe. Take 1lb stoneground wholemeal flour and a handful of salt. Make into a stiff dough, using water. Roll out to about an inch thick. Cut into attractive shapes – Nelson's navy made them round, but you may prefer rectangles or bunny rabbits. Prick with a fork or marlinspike. Bake at 420°C for 30 mins. Visit dentist for comprehensive checkup. Rebake in a very slow oven for 3 days, watching closely for signs of scorching. Cool. Stow. Forget. Serving suggestion: put in canvas bag and hit with hammer.

But 21st-century man does not live by biscuit alone. Man needs to fry stuff, such as sausages, or eggs bought at harbourside WI sales, or mackerel caught over the side. For this, heat is necessary. For my reservations about dual fuel cookers, see above. Gas brings in its train expensive sniffing devices and Corgi-registered bandits. The Minimum favourite is a spirit stove, running on meths. The only downside with this is that the additive that turns the meths blue does not half stink up the cabin. Wait, though. The French do not share the British terror that the public, given free access to mineral spirits, will immediately blind itself by drinking them in pints. They therefore produce a meths without the blue dye. So crack sheets and away to France and buy a couple of gallons. And there at last is the odourless flame burning under *Daisy*'s cast-iron frying pan, in which sizzle a couple of mackerel . . .

Or would have sizzled, on the Night of the Smouldering Visitor, if there had been any mackerel on board. Actually the commissariat was low, consisting of coffee, whisky and a pound of sausages. It was as I say a delightful evening, with the moon in the water and a peachy afterglow on the western horizon. Thanks to the cafetiere and a hint of Glenmorangie, the guest was acting warm, dry and unsinged. I extracted the sausages from the locker and roused out *Daisy*'s barbecue.

This consists of a Mini wheel hub topped with a bit of builder's mesh. To the hub is welded a mild steel prong that fits into the rowlock socket, so the whole apparatus burns about a foot aft of the transom, overhanging the water. I made a small fire of sticks, added a little French spirit, placed organic charcoal on top, and lit it. There followed a great cloud of white smoke, then a sheet of flame and shouting from a voice that I recognized as my own. At some point during this process the barbecue vanished into the deep with a sharp hiss. The flashlight beam illuminated a pound of pork and leek, heavily charred, moving purposefully away down the tide.

'There goes dinner,' said my guest.

He was right, of course. There was nothing else on the boat. Into my mind came a vision of my ship's biscuits, lurking like discs of granite in their locker. 'Tell me,' I said. 'These Reddimeals of yours. What exactly do they taste like?'

PLUMBING

A little while ago we were in the harbour of Craighouse on the Isle of Jura, not that that has anything to do with anything. I had been in Scotland a fortnight, having slid *Daisy* off the trailer at Oban. My acquaintance Dave was there too. He had come round from Mudd Harbour in two hard-fought legs, and by this time he had been in the cruising ground for a day and a half, and reckoned he could spare another four hours before he had to start back.

So there we were, anchored a cable's length apart, when I heard a sort of racket coming from his boat. I unrolled the jib, pulled up the anchor, and sailed over. Dave was in the cockpit, looking far from well and scrubbing his hands in a bucket of bleach. 'Plumbing,' he said, responding to my faintly lifted eyebrow.

'Beer?'

He nodded mutely and grabbed a can like a drowning man clutching at a whole bale of straw. 'It was like this,' he said. 'The pressurised hot-and-cold was making a funny noise, I thought, so I stripped it down.' Through the companionway I could see a five-berth yacht interior knee-deep in dismantled pipework and asbestos lagging. 'But it turned out not to be the hot-and-cold after all,' he said, and buried his face in his hands.

'Head?' I said with a shudder.

'Worse,' he said.

'There is nothing worse.'

'Yes there is,' he said. 'It is called a macerator. You know that gap year crew who jumped ship in Maryport? He must have flushed most of a socket set, the animal.'

There was a pause while we both strove to conquer our gag reflexes. 'And?'

'Beyond me,' said Dave.

'And me,' I said hastily.

'So it's the yard again,' said Dave. 'That little manager bloke who sucks his teeth. "Oo now it wouldn't be fair to meself to give you a quote Mr Strothers, how long is a piece of string, but let's say two K min, sky's the limit really."'

'Dave,' I said sternly. 'What is that thing in front of you?'

'A bucket,' said Dave. 'So?'

'I shall start at the beginning,' I said. 'Come on to the boat. Have a seat. Beer?'

'I think I'll need two,' said Dave.

'Whatever. Now. I do not know if you have been in the far-flung atolls of the Pacific. Over that way you will often see large grey box-shaped vessels flying the Stars and Stripes. These are Facility Ships, full of guns and bombs to facilitate swift military action by the World Superpower. Closer to home, you will find many small vessels containing equally noxious gear, which I call Facilities Ships, the facilities in question being sanitary. Scientists tell us that putting a Baby Blake or (worse) Portapotti into a boat of less than seven metres LOA effectively transforms an ocean gazelle into a mobile lav. As for pressurised water, it is an invention of the Devil and will eat your soul. Behold,' I said with a sweeping gesture of the hand, 'the facilities of the Minimum Boat.'

Dave popped beer number three. 'But there aren't any,' he said.

'Tch,' I said, rummaging in the lazarette. 'Lo!' And I held before him the mahogany bog seat used in conjunction with a bucket by those insufficiently athletic to hang off the mainsheet in the dead of night. I then demonstrated to him the use of the five-gallon water jerrycan with advanced dedicated manual integral pump and plastic washbasin. And I pointed to the mast, where the solar shower hangs dark as a raincloud when we are at anchor.

'But the sun never shines,' said Dave.

'You get a shower one day in three, minimum,' I said. 'If you want to be cleaner than that, go ashore or go on a cruise ship.'

'Hmm,' said Dave, obviously dissatisfied with his lot. 'Gosh, is that the time already? Tide's running south.'

And off he went, down the long wet road round Kintyre and the Irish Sea. While I had lunch, waited for the tide to slack off, and headed north. I had two weeks before the boat went back on the trailer. Someone had said there were a lot of whales by Ardnamurchan this year, and I wanted to have a look at them.

BUCKET

The nights are long and the days are short and *Daisy* is in the barn until varnishing time. And it is the festive season, in which our thoughts go out to the cold and miserable. As Ebenezer Scrooge himself must have known, there is nothing that enhances the warmth of a roaring fire like the sight of an orphan freezing in a snowdrift outside the window.

It is at times like this that it is good to have a pint with my friend Alex and talk about buckets.

The bucket is a crucial bit of the Minimum Boat. In his seminal Minimum book *Sensible Cruising Designs*, the American yacht designer Francis Herreshoff even puts a well-varnished cedar bucket above canvas shoes and coal stoves in the list of essentials. Every boat bucket should of course have a lanyard, eye-spliced to the handle at one end and with a wall knot or other decorative stopper on the other – a hand-loop in a bucket lanyard can pull the small and unwary overboard. Bucket materials are a matter of individual preference. Cedar is now a bit of antique Americana. Galvanized is easy to fill over the side, being heavy enough to sink, and metallic enough to boil a lobster in. Plastic is cheap, plentiful and hygienic, but lacks character.

Probably the greatest exponent of the bucket, and many other facets of Minimum exploring by land and sea, was the great H W Tilman.

Modern explorers tend to have quite a few GPS receivers and satellite phones stashed away in their parkas. When they get stuck on a shrinking floe, they ring up the Canadian Air Force, which drops them another couple of snowmobiles. And if those two go into the sea, hell, you can ring up again and give them your card number, see you in an hour, okay?

This was not the Tilman way. Rumour was his satellite phone, and the seat of his pants his snowmobile. For instance, he was once panning for gold in West Africa when he heard that his friend Eric Shipton was planning to climb Muztagh Ata in the Himalayas. He instantly mounted his bicycle, rode across Africa and took a ship for India. In the Himalayas, he and Shipton worked out that on the traditional expedition, most of the porters were carrying food for the other porters. So the two men scaled the ghastly precipices with a couple of Sherpas. When they ran out of ropes, they used the unrolled turban of a passing tribesman.

You may be asking yourself what this has to do with boats. Good point. Here goes.

Tilman spent WWII causing intense distress to the German army behind its lines. In subsequent years he noticed that Greenland was full of mountains, many of them unclimbed. The best way to get to Greenland, a place inaccessible by bike, seemed to be in a Bristol Channel pilot cutter, so he bought one. To attract crew, he advertised in the personal column of the Times: 'Hands wanted for long voyage in small boat. No pay, no prospects, not much pleasure.' My friend Alex responded to one of these in 1974, was shown his bunk on the starboard side of the forepeak, caught a whiff of Tilman's pipe, and became seasick for a fortnight.

Here the bucket theme returns. In the course of his travail, which was severe, Alex got to know the bucket intimately. He came to realise it was not a mere pail, but a special versatile multipurpose utility vessel, possibly because it was the only one on the boat. He had been sick into it. It lay at the heart of the ship's sanitary systems. And it was a vital part of the *batterie de cuisine*, Tilman's favourite meal being 'a majestic duff in a bucket.'

Alex's sea legs kicked in at last. He flattered himself that the bucket held no further secrets. He had mastered its use in cookery and had a thorough understanding of its other roles. Then one night in the Greenland Strait he was woken by a torrent of icy water. An ice floe had removed a plank from the cutter's starboard bow. And he realised, during all that night and the day that followed, that a bucket was a handy thing to bail with, as well. And that a galvanized one was best when the water had chunks of ice in it.

Oh, look. It is starting to snow. Put another log on the fire. Hot rum? Why not. Buckets? Humbug!

OILSKINS

Very nice place, Norfolk. Sky full of delightful clouds. Beaches covered in birds, seals and cockles. Strong light beloved of painters and air that has come full toss from the Urals bouncing off stately church towers on low cliffs . . .

Sorry. This is supposed to be about boats.

The only problem with Norfolk is that it is hard to get at from the open sea. The Almanac makes remarks about shifting sandbanks, large dangerous wrecks and local knowledge being essential, and the Almanac is dead right. But a minimum boat like *Daisy*, who makes the long and boring bits of passages behind a car, will greet such remarks with a light laugh. So there we were, dried out under a dune waiting for the tide to come in, which was happening at the usual speed i.e. galloping horse, when a geezer I had better call Barry came past.

I am calling him Barry not because it is his real name but because it is short for Barrister, which is what he and quite a lot of people who infest these parts do for a living. He had parked his little gaff-rigged dayboat on the edge of the sea, trudged up the beach, and wandered over to say hello. These things happen, and as long as you keep your eye on the spirit locker they seldom have adverse consequences.

He seemed a nice enough guy, this Barry, very polite about *Daisy*. He admired her home-made ash tiller and teak decks. He agreed that gaff rig was good, centreboards convenient, and outboards less of a strain than inboards. He agreed that in an age where some yachting services are offered by marketing folk with the charitable instincts of Albanian grave robbers, the Minimum Boat is the only way to go. But I noticed that throughout these polite remarks, one of his eyebrows was slightly higher than the other and his eyes kept straying over my person. 'Yes,' he said, as I waxed lyrical about the soft light of paraffin lamps, so much more pleasing than the fluorescent equivalent. 'But what are you *wearing?*'

'Wet gear,' I said. 'State of the art.'

'Ah,' he said.

'Unlike you,' I said. For he was clad in the old Swallows and Amazons rig, viz shorts, khaki, with jersey on top half and weird bobble hat on bonce.

'No need to wear anything but,' he said. 'Brings out the basic toughness in the hardy sons of Britain. And daughters, of course,' he added with a lawyer's instinct for the ever-present danger of equal rights litigation. 'If it gets cold, put on another jersey. Think of Paul Elvstrom, one of Britain's hottest competitive sailors of a generation just passed. Used to wear, I dunno, four, five jerseys. Before he went racing he used to dip himself in the sea so the whole lot were soaking wet. They weighed so much he could hardly stagger into the boat. But when he sat the boat out, that extra few stone brought it bolt upright and he roared past one and all.'

'Ah,' I said. It sounded a bit like cheating to me, but of course Barry was a lawyer, so he probably wouldn't have recognized the concept.

'Whereas you,' said this fearless advocate, 'bang on and on month after month about the Minimum Boat, but you are wearing *plastic.*'

'In a way,' I said, pulling up my hood, for a cloud had rolled over the sun, and it had begun to rain heavily. I saw this hardy son of Britain looking about him for an umbrella or perhaps a bus shelter, and finding none. 'But,' I said, speaking slowly, for I am a sadist at heart, 'I am living on this boat, and the cabin is too small to swing a mouse let alone a cat, and drying clothes is out of the question. On the Minimum Boat,' I said, 'once you are wet you stay wet. So what I am wearing are Henri Lloyd Offshore Breathables or something. They have got so many pockets you will still be finding packets of fags three years after you have stopped smoking, and they cost nearly as much as a house. But they are as dry as most houses and drier than mine, which was built in the Middle Ages and has holes in the roof. And on my feet I am wearing those boots made out of leather and Gore-Tex, because on the Minimum Boat it may be some days before you take your boots off, and if you have got rubber on your feet birds will be falling out of the sky. The boots are very expensive, but frankly worth it.'

Barry made a sceptical noise, then looked at his watch, which was half full of water. 'Gosh,' he said, 'is that the time already? I must be going.'

'No hurry,' I said.

'Wife,' said Barry. 'Secretary of Golf Club. Coming round for her sherry.'

'Round?'

'To the cottage.'

'Oh the *cottage*,' I said. 'With a tumble drier?'

'Naturally.'

'Ah well,' I said. 'Bon voyage.'

I watched his little brown sail slide away down the creek into the rain, towards the cottage, where the clothes would be dried all warm and fluffy. Then I took off my wet gear and stuffed it under the sprayhood and went below into the minimum cabin and thanked the Lord for freedom from Golf Club secretaries. And thought, minimum boat, maximum oilskins.

PRACTICAL MATTERS
NAVIGATION

In the Cannon and Midshipman the other night, my friend Ernie revealed that he was off to do his Yachtmaster (Shorebased). My other friend Dave, who has got a Day Skipper and has sailed round the world a couple of times, said he was disillusioned by the RYA syllabus. This was a result of his meeting trainee Yachtmasters (Ocean) doing qualifying miles on crewed charters and their sextant work on the deck of the Plymouth-Santander ferry. The talk then turned to the subject of Minimum Navigation.

True Minimum Navigation was practised by the likes of Uffa Fox and Blondie Hasler. Hasler is said to have made it a point of honour never to use a corrected chart. Fox is said to have stayed in his bunk during the entire first tack of a windy down-Channel passage. At 0200 his head appeared in the companionway, and he took a deep sniff of racing air. 'Bad drains and cheap scent,' he said. 'Must be Cherbourg. Ready about, lee-oh.'

The state-of-the-art form of Minimum Navigation is to carry four GPS sets. But navigation and pilotage should be belt, braces and superglue. So backup systems are vital. Ernie started to drone on about dead reckoning and buoy lists, and quite right too. But the talk soon moved into more Minimum waters. Mudd Harbour pilotage has always involved a system of transits: put the Red Lion in line with the Eel and Strumpet and your course will allow you to see in at the saloon bar window of the Anchor and check out the guest beer. Some transits are unofficial, and made up as you go along. Others are so well established that you can bet the Vikings used them as they came into soundings, spotted the local monastery and started patting their pockets for matches.

The conversation then turned to some dodges that are currently unfashionable, perhaps because they are laborious. Dave spoke warmly of three-point bearings taken using a sextant on its side. Ernie mentioned arming the lead with tallow to take seabed samples – most Minimum Boats carry leadlines, though tallow can be hard to come by, butter is too buttery, and jam dissolves, but you can usually achieve something with a bit of forethought and some candle wax.

Off soundings, navigation can be actively poetic. Assuming you have dropped the sextant and the GPSs have been stolen by pirates, you can use birds, said Dave. If the sea is laced with Cory's shearwaters and nothing else, you are at least three days from land, and (he claimed) the same goes for albatrosses in the Southern Hemisphere. As the land approaches, you get young gannets, wearing the dazed expression signalling that they have no idea how they got this far from home. Behind them are older gannets, looking anxiously about them for mackerel shoals and lost children. As you close the coast the fulmars kick in, gliding stiff-winged along the wavetops. Past the fulmars are the gulls and guillemots and razorbills. Cormorants and shags are a sign of imminent landfall. Greenshanks piping in darkness and fog are a sign that your landfall is going to be both imminent and challenging, possibly involving the lifeboat. Thrushes, blackbirds and robins are a sign that it is far too late.

I am personally an advocate of the Polynesian method. Polynesian charts are made of bamboo strips which symbolise the direction of waves, studded with little cowrie shells indicating the position of stars. Using these, Pacific navigators regularly achieved amazing feats of pinpoint navigation, even while blindfolded by sceptical missionaries. It is not however at all an easy technique for anyone not born in a canoe, and is unlikely to find its way onto the RYA syllabus.

The talk was by now getting extremely poetic. We spoke of examination of the sea itself, a method loved by the more spiritual type of French navigator eg Bernard Moitessier. Sargassum weed and flat calm mean you are south of Bermuda. Big white islands of ice mean . . . well, you get the picture.

There is of course a very, very reliable method, and one that we were all able to endorse. It involves sailing across a stretch of water until you make landfall. You then coast in a likely direction until you see a port. Enter the port and step ashore. To discover the port's name, ask a policeman.

This winter we will be doing our RYA Discovering New Continents (Shorebased) Certificate.

ANCHORAGES

PEYTON

I went into Mudd Marina the other day, because they have got a tap there, and if you are really quick you can fill up the water breaker and get away before a Berthing Master with the instincts of a Mafia bookie charges you £17 for a short stay. As I left, sloshing pleasantly, I saw Barry on his Baywatch 37 (metres, not feet) getting ready for sea.

I put the helm down and went over, for Barry's friend Chantelle has a lovely smile. 'Off to the Continong for wines?' I said.

'Nah,' said Barry, looking shifty. 'Thought we'd, you know, spend a night on the anchor. Listen to the birds and that.'

Barry's idea of a bird worth listening to is Sheryl Crow, so ornithology seemed unlikely to be the reason for this behaviour. A more probable reason was that nowadays it costs £6000 to fill the Baywatch's tanks, and Barry is in houses, or possibly banking, so he is on the lookout for cheap options at all times. 'Anchor?' I said. 'Me too. Lovely. Where?'

'What about Nailground Bay?'

Well, Nailground is charming if a little exposed, with a long white beach and a pub. But it has disadvantages. One, minor, is a strong infestation of galloping nudists in the dunes. Another, more severe, is that on a breezy night there will be four hundred boats in there, few with holding tanks, so the brown stuff on the beach is unlikely to be driftwood. And the third, most significant of all, was that the forecast was grim and equinoctical. I said, 'Personally, I am going to Legg.'

'Me too, yeah,' said Barry hurriedly.

So off for Legg we set.

Legg is partly sheltered by a low sandstone cliff topped with woods that comb the malice out of the breeze. A decent anchor will hold anything there. As I laid out *Daisy*'s oversized Bruce in 2m of water I noticed Barry far too close. He bundled a thing like a bent teaspoon overboard with a remarkably short lump of chain, then scuttled aft to where Chantelle was knocking up banana daiquiris. 'Got swinging room?' I said.

Barry frowned at me over the rim of his glass. 'Games room, billiard room, course,' he said. 'But swinging, well, Chantelle's not really into that scene, worse luck.' He went below for a bubble bath. Sighing, I pulled up *Daisy*'s anchor and reset it a safe distance away.

Soon after that, Torquil the Latin teacher came in with his 50ft Nicholson, and the cliff resounded to the merry clack of the gypsy as form 4b of St Donuts veered several shackles of chain. Finally in came a Mirror dinghy, which turned out to be Dave in his tender. Dave lives aboard his sloop, chained to an anchor that has been down for so long that there is no way of getting it up without a floating crane, an operation Dave cannot currently finance. So we nattered about this and that as a slaty roof of cloud slid across the sky. 'Here it comes,' said Dave. 'Off I go.' And off he went, chased by the first drops of rain.

'Barbie?' called Chantelle, waving a raw bass.

I declined, for I sensed that there might soon be other fish to fry.

The tide started to ebb, and the barometer chased it into the cellar, and the sound of Torquil's pupils singing Etruscan glees was drowned by the rising howl of the wind. To this was soon added another howling, unmistakably human. Putting my head out of the hatch, I saw the dark shadow of Barry's Baywatch dragging briskly down the wind, her owner struggling on the foredeck in a rain-lashed silk dressing gown. From the other side came the whimper and clank of form 4b laying out more chain. *Daisy* was pitching jerkily in the chop, in a manner not dangerous but distinctly uncomfortable. It was time for a Minimum Manoeuvre. I started the engine and motored into the ripple under the cliff's lee until the nose touched sand. The tide ebbed. *Daisy* took the ground. The world slid away for eight hours, accompanied by the howl of the weather and the occasional bloody gleam of the flares Barry seemed to be firing. My last conscious thought was a Minimum one. There are unsafe anchorages and safe anchorages, it went. But the safest anchorage of all is on dry land.

SELF STEERING

The Rev and I have been on our annual cruise in company. These cruises last ten days or so, and are conducted off the West Coast of Scotland, singlehanded, in identical boats. If you are sailing identical boats with same-sized crews, the person who gets to the night's destination first is the person who has the boat in the best trim. It is not exactly racing, but everyone likes to keep up.

In normally-crewed boats, helming is the job of the helmsman, and trim is the job of the crew or throttler. Singlehanding is different. So there I was, some distance off Skye, steering with my foot while I cranked in a few more millimetres on the gaff to get an extra nanoknot, when the foot slipped and *Daisy*'s weather helm shot her up into the wind, everything flapping. As I hauled her back on course, the Rev slid past with the grace of a figure skater, sitting on the foredeck, waving with one hand and holding in the other a cup of freshly made tea. From his open hatch came a waft of blue fumes produced, by the smell of it, by frying bacon. How had he managed to leave the tiller for long enough to organize all these things?

I followed his ruler-straight wake into Badachro, and found him peacefully at anchor in that green and pleasant spot. 'What kept you?' he said.

'This and that,' I said, dropping an anchor and coming alongside him, for it was the cocktail hour.

He looked over at my boat, and a shadow crossed his brow. 'I was going to say, have a drink,' he said. 'But I perceive that you will be wanting to clean up your cockpit. There are bits of sandwich all over the deck and if I am not mistaken that is your reefing line mixed up with the traveller outhaul and the mainsheet. Accident looking for a place to happen,' said the Rev.

Sanctimonious, I thought. But as so often, the Rev had a point. My cockpit was indeed a mess, and his was not. His halyards were neatly coiled on their cleats, the mainsheet was arranged in a frankly exhibitionistic Flemish coil, and what I could see of his cabin looked as if it had been tidied by a large and highly trained domestic staff. 'I presume,' I said, 'that you have been lucky enough to secure the assistance of angels. Or can it be that you have rigged up a self steering device using string, so you can tidy up, cook snacks and generally have a life away from the drudgery of the tiller?'

'No angels, yea, nor have I used string,' said the Rev. 'I have got a tillerpilot, and very nice too.'

'A tillerpilot?' I said, shocked. 'But we are Minimum Boats.'

'All right,' said the Rev. 'You tell me one thing more minimum than a tillerpilot, and you can have next Sunday's collection plate, buttons and all. Naturally, one does all the hand steering one wants to do. But when one wishes to trim a sail, one engages the magic box and trims away until the boat is fairly flying. When one wishes to navigate, one does not have to heave-to off a nasty lee shore in a breeze suddenly blowing Force 7 to consult charts while the rocks surge ever closer. One presses the magic button, freeing both hands, takes impeccable bearings, and picks up without fuss or effort the first of the perches marking the channel through the legendary maelstrom guarding Poll Creadha. And when it comes to finding time for tidying cockpits, frying bacon, and making flower arrangements in cabins, the autopilot is without peer and without rival, provided a sharp lookout is kept at all times.'

'Hmm,' I said.

'Electric cabin lights are a waste of time and most unhomely,' said the Rev. 'Electronic charts are for gadget freaks, radar is for masochists and hot water comes from kettles, not calorifiers. But with tillerpilots, minimum cruising becomes a joy instead of a scrabble.

'Hmm,' I said again, and I meant it to sting.

But a seed once planted must grow. I am on the boat now. I am sitting in the hatch, maintaining a watch, heeled gently to starboard. *Daisy*'s sails are meticulously trimmed, and you could eat your dinner off any part of her immaculately tidy cockpit. At the after end of said cockpit the tillerpilot wheezes away. I have been sailing, and while I have been sailing I have been writing these words. Any minute now we will be making landfall, my tillerpilot and me.

CHARTS

Barry has been at it again. There we all were, Dave who has the long keel sloop he still can't sell, and Torquil who has the great big Nicholson and teaches classics at St Donuts, having a sunset wine in Donkey Bay after a nice evening sail in *Daisy*. Then there was a rumble of twin diesels and round the headland streaked a Baywatch 37 (metres, not feet) that we all recognized as Barry's *Capitalist Tool*. It hurtled towards us, went head to wind and dropped anchor. Torquil said, 'Something is going on.'

'What?' I said, extracting Cork 3.

'His curtains are drawn.'

They were, too. Furthermore the tuna tower was deserted. The Baywatch dug in its anchor and stopped engines with a sound like an earthquake knocking off for lunch. 'Here he comes,' said Dave.

We composed our faces into expressions of quiet disapproval. The Baywatch excreted a tender from its transom, and across came Barry, who is in metals now, and Chantelle, who is usually in not much, tonight being no exception. 'Ello boys!' cried Chantelle gaily, scissoring aboard *Daisy* with a lightning-flash of thigh. Barry followed, plonking a magnum of Bollinger on the cockpit table.

'Nice curtains,' said Dave.

'Oh, them old things,' said Chantelle. 'Baz made me draw them – '

'Hrahumph,' said Barry. 'Curtains? Drawn? So they are. Never noticed. You don't, when you are using Acme Large Scale One Metre Accurate Garmolene Plotmatic with IFF and Autoanchor instead of paper charts.'

Torquil sniffed. 'Charts?' he said. 'Personally I am with Blondie Hasler and Uffa Fox, heroes of past yachting. Charts are scarcely necessary, because I know the bottom of the sea as I know my own. Updated charts are a mark of low moral fibre. Navigation is best done by nose, i.e. garlic for southern Abroad, herrings for northern Abroad, and splendid roast beef for dear old England.'

As you can imagine, this caused a bit of a silence. Dave broke it. 'Owning a long keel sloop like mine is an expensive business,' he said. 'So I have been economizing by using the *AA Road Atlas of Britain*, like many a seafarer before me. There are a surprising number of lighthouses marked on it, plus nuclear power stations and ferry routes.' He drained his glass. 'I am using the 2001 edition at the moment, but I shall be updating if successful in the bidding for a 2006 edition on eBay.'

'Course you shall,' said Chantelle, patting his hand, for she is kind as well as beautiful, and hates to see a man feeling inadequate (though actually Dave never feels inadequate, and the chances are he was aiming for the hand-patting all along). She looked up at me under her lashes. 'I bet you got lovely charts,' she said.

'Indeed,' I said. 'Naturally I spend most of the winter evenings updating old charts, adding new developments such as the coasts of America. But when I buy new ones, I buy them in folios. Other sailing countries have long been used to the idea of issuing charts in these handy and economical packages. British chart manufacturers have resisted the trend, fearing it will dent their vast profits. Finally, they have cracked. Much of the South Coast, the Med and the Caribbean are now available in folio form. For the Minimum Boater who wishes to navigate in the rain, some are available printed on tough plastic – ideal for the half-open boat, such as *Daisy*.'

'Mmm,' said Chantelle, stifling a yawn. 'Really?'

'Fog's coming in,' said Torquil.

It was, thick and wet and black as the inside of a cow.

'You can get home with yer new charts,' said Barry. There was a crash. 'Oops. There goes the bottle. My fault.'

Another advantage of plastic charts on the Minimum Boat is that they are multifunctional, i.e. ideal for ladling broken glass into the gash, though this lot went unreadable in the process. 'Never mind,' said Torquil. 'We'll go home seat of the pants, lead line and compass, jolly good show.'

'Nah,' said Chantelle. 'We'll tow ya, innit, Baz? And you can drive this time. Butterfingers.'

'Gnagn,' said Barry.

We rigged an alongside tow, settled Barry on his dank tuna tower, and opened another bottle in his walnut saloon.

'Hope it's not too much trouble,' I called up the hatch into the wet black night.

'Fingers crossed,' said Dave.

'Oo you are awful,' said Chantelle.

FISHING

We like a bit of fishing on *Daisy*. Tooling along off the coast of Scotland, three knots, light airs, broad reach. One hand for the tiller, one for the line. Land a jagged shadow on the eastern horizon, beer nestled in a coil of jib sheet on the nice teak deck. Pretty tough, the seafaring life.

A couple of trawlers were moving across the sea. The mind drifted away. Most of the Western Approaches has been trawled at least once in the past year, which is why Deke the Diver reckons that much of the seabed looks like a ploughed field, except with fewer weeds. Thank you, politicians who donated British fisheries to foreigners.

Yank, yank on the line. Steer with the foot. Haul with the hands. Charming mackerel, lunch size. Gut, split, press out bones and fry. Corporate executives are looting the seas; one fish is enough for the minimum fisherman. Homeward ho.

'Fish?' said Harry, when I anchored next to his antique fishing boat. 'Only one? Look at this.' He shoved his bucket over: yellow plastic, half-full of blue-green corpses. 'I was using feathers,' he said. 'Twenty-six fish.' He waited for the applause.

'So when are you going to eat them?' I said.

'Eat? Oh,' said Harry, with the air of one who had not thought of that.

'Like the Native Americans of the Pacific seaboard, you must love your quarry,' I said, and gave him a brief lecture on the evils of catching more than you can eat. Somewhere near the end, a brown sail came round the point. It seemed to be a Drascombe, and it was as crowded as Captain Bligh's launch with people in their early twenties. Everyone was singing, and I saw one of the girls pass one of the other girls a bottle of whisky. This is the kind of thing that happens in Scotland. 'Oh, look,' said Harry. 'It's the Youth.'

It was indeed, dear friends and relations all of them. 'More whisky!' they cried, sweeping neatly alongside. Fenders went down, warps came across and they noticed the bucket. 'Fish!' they cried. 'Lovely!'

'Thank goodness they came,' said Harry, passing them the bucket. 'Oh my God.'

For a long knife was dissecting the fish laid out on the wooden top of the Drascombe's centreboard case. The girls heaved out of the stern locker bottles of soy sauce, wasabe radish and ginger. 'Banzai! Sashimi!' cried the youngest and the blondest of the girls, dunking a slab in the condiments and eating it raw.

'Great,' said Harry, who likes his sashimi fried but hates to show weakness. He ate one fish, then another. The Drascombe mob did likewise, washing it down with great draughts of my whisky. The level of fish in the bucket sank.

'That must make you feel better,' I said.

'In a way,' said Dave, looking slightly greenish. 'Try some.'

'Allergic,' I said, for in my view one mackerel a day is the adult dose. 'Can I have the bones?'

The Youth handed over the guts and skeletons, burping faintly. 'Waste not, want not,' I said, continuing my policy of revolting smugness. 'Actually I shall be using them as bait.' Expanding my portable lobster pots (the concertina type with the net entrances, not the inferior fan type with the hard plastic ring) I baited them with mackerel skeletons. Then I sailed them out to the skerries, went head to wind in the blue scend and dropped them overboard, returning as the sun went down to join Harry and the Youth in a selection of Everly Brothers songs.

In the morning, I went to haul the pots. In Pot 1 was a small lobster, which I threw back, and eleven green crabs. In Pot 2 was a ruddy great conger, which flopped out of the pot and chased me two circuits of the cockpit, gnashing its jagged teeth. Taking refuge on the bowsprit, I considered my options. If I had had a gun, I would have shot it. If I had had an axe, I would have chopped it up. As it was, I had a sail bag. So I made my way aft, tripped over the jib sheet, hit my head on the boom, grabbed the fish through the bag, cursed it horribly and flung it over the side.

'Oi!' said Harry, who had come out to watch. 'Love your quarry, innit?'

I pretended not to hear him.

TENDER

PEYTON

We sailed jib-only past the sunken rocks into the anchorage at Scavaig on Skye. And there was a 40ft Swedish boat, with a mauve person on the foredeck, blowing up a tender. It made you feel hot just to look at him. And it started the usual train of thought about Minimum Tenders.

A tender carries stores and people. Children will use it to learn to row, sail and cross imaginary oceans. Most people use inflatables – easy to stow, tow beautifully, stable as the Rock of Gibraltar, and can in emergency be used as liferafts, MOB recovery systems or giant fenders. But they are boring to inflate and annoying to row, so it is tempting to put a small outboard on the back end. Which is fine, until the children get hold of it. Sudden catastrophic vulcanism apart, there is no greater horror in an anchorage than an eight-year-old with a 2hp Honda.

Rigid tenders have their advocates. They row well. And even if you can't fit them on deck you can always tow them. Once, no self-respecting cruising family would undertake its summer hols without a 17ft clinker dinghy behind its 27ft yacht. Dinghy running into transom? Hang a bucket out the back end or tow it on a bridle. Two and a half knots is as fast as anyone needs go, old boy. Rome wasn't built in a day you know.

The ideal rigid tender is light, preferably a pram and preferably Norwegian. Failing the Norwegian option, Minimum Boaters including me have built 6ft stitch-and-glue prams on the kitchen table. The upside of this is that they are cheap and they carry a lot of weight while remaining stable. The downside is that while in build they can cause domestic strife by sticking to the soup.

A rigid tender has the further advantage of being scullable. This dying art is practised with a single oar whose loom rests in that notch on the transom. The wrist-flexing that imparts the required figure-of-eight motion to the oar blade takes about twenty minutes to learn. A Chinese variant is the yuloh, a sculling oar with a blade bent at 12° to the oar loom, its handle connected by a lanyard to a thwart. Heaving to and fro on this lanyard produces the figure-of-eight motion. Apparently the Chinese propel 50ft sampans to and fro with these objects –

Wait a minute. Wait a *minute*, I thought a year or two ago. What if the Minimum Tender is *no tender at all? Daisy* is 19ft LOD, and weighs perhaps a ton and a quarter in commission. I hastened to bolt a rowlock to the transom. Then, dropping a 15ft oar into the rowlock, I began to scull. It was a slow start, but once a ton or so starts moving through the water it keeps going. And in the end the bow touched Scavaig's granite shore with a soft bump.

You will however have spotted the hitch. The wind was blowing onshore. Unlike most tenders, *Daisy* does not pull up the beach. She needs anchoring off. French people solve this problem by dropping an anchor with a block attached on the way in, having previously run a long line from the boat's Samson post through the sheave. They hang on to the line, paying it out as necessary. Once everyone is ashore, they give a heave, and out glides the boat onto the anchor. *Voila*!

In theory.

What actually happens is that the sheave gets snarled up with the line. So when you try to haul the boat out you haul the anchor home instead, and when you try to haul the boat in the ruddy thing just sits twenty yards off the beach and sneers at you. *Merde*!

Use a tripping line instead. Take one anchor, with warp attached to boat. Position anchor on foredeck with long light line attached to its crown. Give the boat a sensitive yet mighty shove into the offing, releasing line as it goes. When all motion has ceased, give a sharp tug. The anchor will plummet off the foredeck and into the sea, where it will do its stuff. Attach line to boulder for future reference. Go and wallow in the Scavaig river, which runs over black rock that heats it on a sunny day to the temperature of bathwater. On return, haul in tripping line and scull out to anchorage.

Or get a tow from a Swedish person with an outboard on his inflatable. I know I did.

GRACIOUS SEAFARING
FLAG ETIQUETTE

We were in Mudd Marina, lounging in the pure teak cockpit of the Admiral's Swan, viewing the passing scene. 'The Custom of the Sea,' said the Admiral, 'is what separates Man from the Animals.'

'Zat so?' said my friend Barry, gazing proudly upon the Union Jack fluttering from the topmost aerial of his Baywatch 37 (metres, not feet), tied up on the outside of a large raft.

'Tchah,' said the Admiral.

'I like a bit of bunting,' said Barry. 'Colourful.'

Barry is a kind man, but he does not do Etiquette. And sometimes it is hard not to conclude that he is right. 'We pride ourselves on our commitment to the fine old delirium of messing about in boats,' says the website of the Mudd Harbour Yacht Club. 'But we do insist on the wearing of blazers and ties in the bar; no trousers for the ladies obviously.'

Barry and I and the Admiral watched a perfectly-dressed member of the Yacht Club step out of the bar wearing black-soled shoes, march through a puddle of waste oil, then stump across the cockpits of two rafted-up yachts and onto the boat of a Yacht Club colleague. Lighting a Burma cheroot, the member disappeared down the companionway. 'Tch,' said Barry.

'Quite,' said the Admiral.

'Unforgivable really,' said Barry. 'Doesn't ask permission to come aboard. Black soles on the decks. Oil everywhere. Stumps straight through the cockpits instead of tiptoeing over the foredeck. And smoking below decks. Yuck,' said Barry.

'Quite. Burmese cheroot. Ghastly,' said the Admiral. 'I mean why not a Havana?'

It was time to intervene. 'You were saying, Admiral,' I said. 'The Custom of the Sea.'

'Ah yes,' said the Admiral. 'Flag etiquette. Colourful, tchah. Crucially important backbone of the nation. It is an offence under the Merchant Shipping Act involving a fine of up to £1,000 to do anything other than what I am about to describe. Ensign first. If you are an ordinary British yacht, you fly a red ensign as close to the back end as you can get it, meaning from the transom, or the gaff peak if your boom is long enough to foul the staff, or off the backstay if there is no staff. If you are a superior British yacht, you may belong to a club with a warrant to fly a defaced Blue Ensign. This is flown only when the owner is on board, carrying a warrant, and only with the Club burgee at the masthead. White ensigns are flown by the Royal Yacht Squadron, the Royal Navy, and by God when he moves on the face of the waters. The Union Jack is never flown, except by the Royal Navy. Ensigns go up at 0800 in summer, 0900 in winter, and come down at 2100 or sunset, whichever is the later. Did you yawn, Barry?'

'Zz,' said Barry.

'Next, courtesy flags and burgees,' said the Admiral, steaming on. 'The burgee is flown at the masthead. The courtesy flag of a country in whose waters you are sailing is flown from a halyard rigged to the starboard spreaders. No flag should be flown above a courtesy flag. This can lead to a clash if you wish to fly a club burgee from the spreaders, as no other flag should be flown above a club burgee. Some people nowadays fly their burgee or club flag from the port spreaders. This,' said the Admiral, scowling, 'is very, very reprehensible. As is the display of saltires, skulls and crossbones, Welsh dragons and Tibetan wind fish. Still with me?'

'Wha?' said Barry.

'Good,' said the Admiral. 'This brings me to House Flags, Ensigns Flown Inverted as Signals of Distress, and the correct order for Dressing Overall – '

The click of stilettoes sounded on the dock. Barry looked up. 'Ullo Chantelle!' he cried.

'Ello Bazza!' cried a pneumatic vision in linen mini skirt and universal tan.

'Scuse me,' said Barry, scrambling for the dock. We watched him remove his and Chantelle's shoes, take off the long warps attaching the Baywatch to the pontoon, ask permission of all owners to come aboard, tiptoe across the foredecks of the raft, settle Chantelle into a deep leather armchair in the cockpit, cast off and rumble into the offing.

As night fell, the Admiral and I passed *Capitalist Tool* anchored in a secluded bay. A Union Jack flapped proudly from her tuna tower, and from the staff at her back end flapped a large pair of boxer shorts, surmounted by a set of tiny lace knickers.

'Animals!' puffed the Admiral, dipping his ensign to a passing aircraft carrier, which ignored him.

It was hard to agree.

ONBOARD ENTERTAINMENT

We were tied up under the Dromedaris in Hoorn, jewel of the Ijsselmeer, a town in which nothing much has changed since Rembrandt, loading groceries off the quay. There was a big fat yacht in front, German ensign, man on the coachroof. He was waggling a TV aerial. 'Anything?' he yelled down the hatch, in German obviously.

'Nothing,' cried a female voice from the bowels.

'Now?'

'The screen gives snow. Hurry, Dieter, it begins!'

A roar of static, faintly mixed with the theme from *Hollyoaks*. Closing my ears, I went below to stow the groceries.

On-board entertainment on the Minimum Boat does not include TV. There are other things to do. Some people like varnishing. This is what the French think the English spend all their time doing (what the English think the French spend all their time doing is different, and hinges on the French penchant for cruising seven to a Folkboat). I am not a keen varnisher during the summer cruise. The weather is invariably too hot or too cold or too wet or too dry. Besides which it gets in the way of the tasting of fine wines, which in moderation is certainly most diverting.

Excessive wine tasting, however, can interfere with the accurate playing of musical instruments. On *Daisy*, instruments are important

– the cabin is about the size of a matchbox, but there is always room for guitar stowage. Playing music warms the heart. It also pleases seals and keeps gulls off the rig. It may lead to lasting friendships in some anchorages, blizzards of flung bottles in others. As so often in music, sensitivity is all.

When sea conditions make instruments impossible, unaccompanied singing is all right. Minimum boats with outboards are in a specially privileged position. A two-stroke Mariner is the ideal drone accompaniment to folk songs, particularly (for some reason) John Hardy, John Wesley Harding, John Riley, Where Have All the Flowers John, and indeed just about any other song with John in the title.

Not everyone is keen on music, of course. Many are content with silence. Sporting types may prefer ad hoc games. When sailing downwind, it is pleasant to rig a lavatory seat on the end of the boom and throw potatoes through it. Slightly more intellectual cruising yachtspeople may prefer talking books, downloadable from sites like www.audible.co.uk. My cousin Katy certainly does. I know, because I have watched her sail singlehanded into a Scottish whirlpool, deaf to my frantic squawks on the VHF and blinded by tears induced by the wrenching pathos of *Anna Karenina*.

But the true minimum on-board entertainment system is the ship's library. Obviously there will be a few cubic feet of charts, almanacs and pilot books. The rest is calculated to deepen the enjoyment of the boat and the watery substances on which it swims. *Daisy*'s bookshelf contains an *Admiralty Manual of Seamanship* for 1930, for general interest and to make the reader thankful for the advancement of science since the days of manila ropes and flax canvas (Tom Cunliffe's *RYA Manual of Seamanship* is a modern equivalent). Naturally there is the *Ashley Book of Knots*, a book of stunning beauty containing instructions for some 7,000 knots, the ideal companion for a rainy day in a boat full of string. Then there are the Collins field guides to birds and fish, and miscellaneous identification manuals for the sea and its inhabitants.

Given the uncertainties of life at sea, a spot of Holy Writ can be a great comfort. And a handful of novels is useful, not forgetting at least one hefty classic to beguile a stormbound three days, and a James Michener thousand-pager, just the right size to use as a pillow for forty winks in the cockpit. Finally, for night sailing it is crucial to have a copy of Stephen Hawking's *Brief History of Time*. After midnight, the crew on watch reads this book one paragraph at a time to the helmsman. It is then the helmsman's task to explain to the crew what the paragraph meant. When and if both parties agree, the crew reads the next paragraph, and the exercise is repeated. Three paragraphs a night is the world record; but at least everyone stays awake.

Actually, what with all this it is a wonder how most Minimum Boat people fit any sailing in. Except when German-dubbed *Hollyoaks* is wafting strength ten from the boat ahead; when it makes perfect sense to point the bowsprit at the open Ijsselmeer, pile on the canvas, and get as far away as possible as fast as you can.

LANGUAGE

PEYTON

It was a springlike sort of evening. We were all sitting on the deck of Torquil's gigantic Nicholson alongside the Town Quay, watching someone silhouetted against the sunset just below the maintop of a visiting square-rigger. 'Honestly will you look at that,' said Torquil. 'The silly fool has got his euphroes in way of his catharpins. How does he think anyone's going to get at the futtocks?'

We all went 'Hmm,' fingering our chins and wagging our heads sagely.

Then a mighty shadow slid alongside with a sound like a thunderstorm in a dustbin. Lines snaked out of the darkness onto Torquil's deck. 'Hullo boys!' said a voice. And we realised that the shadow was the Baywatch 37 (metres, not feet) of our old friend Barry, and the voice was the voice of his lovely partner Chantelle.

Well, he got bow and stern lines on, and a reunion commenced. Someone mentioned Barry's business affairs, rumoured to be in a bit of a muddle what with one thing and another. 'A significant refocusing of revenue streams has occurred,' he said loftily. 'Certain anomalies have now been rationalised and agreements with stakeholders reached. Anyone want any fags, cheap?'

We understood the last bit, but what had gone before might as well have been medieval Greek. We did more chin stroking and hmming, though, and I think Torquil even managed a sage nod.

'Right,' said Dave, who can change a subject quicker than Sam Davies can change headsails in a line squall. 'Well, good to see you, Barry and Chantelle, but are you sure you want to put that figure eight on the bitts? Personally I would feel happier with a trawler hitch. Otherwise you'll be on deck at four bells clapping a magnus hitch on the warp and it'll be the Devil to pay and no pitch hot unless I greatly err in my assessment of Chantelle's need for eight hours of the uninterrupted.'

'Hot bitch *what?*' said Chantelle, eyes snapping fury.

Here the conversation became general as everyone tried to change the subject at exactly the same moment. As so often, it fell to my lot to calm Chantelle, using Chilean chardonnay in the Harbour View Bar. 'I still hate it when they use all that language,' she said. 'I got no idea what they're on about, except someone is always going to start shouting any minute.'

'Yes, yes, there, there,' I said. 'Come for a nice sail tomorrow. The forecast's lovely.'

'In your little tiny boat?' she said. 'Oo.' Next morning did indeed dawn warm and springlike, and there she was, wearing low heels specially for the occasion. 'Why don't you sit down on the left hand side while I pull this string and untie those ropes?' I said. Then up with the main and I let go the jib furling line and hauled on the sheet, and the jib backed, and the nose came off the quay, and as we gathered way I let go the stern line, which I had naturally had on a slip. And the chuckle of the wake became a roar, and the quay slid by. 'Lovely,' said Chantelle, flushed with delight.

'There's a bottle of wine in the cupboard downstairs,' I said.

'Left hand cupboard or right hand cupboard?' said Chantelle.

'Both,' I said, evading a car ferry, for it was the stand-on vessel.

'Splicing the mainbrace, eh?' said Chantelle, swigging Sancerre. 'Hee hee. Oo I hate sea language.'

Naturally I did not agree, but this was Chantelle, so there was no sense arguing. As luck would have it we were at that moment passing Barry's boat. Barry was descending a companion ladder onto what you would have to call the promenade deck, carrying a tin of red paint.

'Yoo hoo!' cried Chantelle. 'Ahoy, Bazza!'

Barry looked round. His foot missed the last step of the ladder. He went flat on the teak. The red paint sailed through the air, landed in the exact centre of quarter of an acre of perfect dove-grey planking, and burst like a bomb.

'@££$$%%^&,' said Barry. '*&$£2@. Oh, @£$!!!**'

'Temper,' said Chantelle.

But I thought: you can keep your catharpins and your asset streams and your magnus hitches and your stand-on vessels. What Barry is speaking face down on his paint-splattered acres of teak is the true language of the British sailorman.

SHOUTING

It was one of those long summer Mudd Harbour evenings, with peace spreading over the deeps and creeks like a bright vapour. There we were, me and *Daisy* and my acquaintance Frank, tacking smooth and dignified up East Deep, listening to the birds and the beasts. When suddenly there was a rattle and a roar and a smallish yacht piled past on a dead run with the spinnaker in the well-known hourglass configuration. 'Lazy sheet!' screamed the helmsman to his lady crew, who was approximately one metre away from him. 'LAZY SHEET! PORT NOT STARBOARD MORON! LET GO THE LEE RUNNER. NO THE LEE RUNNER CRETIN, IT IS AMAZING YOU CAN WORK OUT HOW TO BREATHE.'

These remarks must have caused him to lose concentration, for the boat jibed, bringing the boom smartly onto the weather runner, which broke, and the top of the mast fell forward, and the boat slewed out of the channel and went aground. The yelling continued. The crew clambered into the tender and started rowing briskly into the offing. She appeared to be weeping.

'What's her problem, then?' said Frank.

'No idea,' I said, lying. 'The shouting, perhaps?'

'Everyone shouts on boats,' said Frank. 'To make themselves heard above wind and wave, like. Plus surveys show that just as you cannot learn to ride a horse without falling off nine times you cannot learn to sail without being called an effing moron lots.'

I flicked a speck of dust off the irreproachable Goretex of my cuff. 'I do not remember hearing anything about this at the RYA,' I said.

'I went on this Dazed Kipper course,' said Frank. 'And there was this instructor who kept a copy of *Mein Kampf* by his bunk and shouted all the time. He said the shouting kept us safe and that sailing is a sort of military thing to do so it is reasonable to enforce discipline using the voice.'

'Frank,' I said, 'if your instructor called you personally a moron it seems he had a point. If you want squarebashing, join the Territorial Army. I and my many cousins were bellowed at while learning to sail in infancy. Those of us who went into therapy swiftly learned the old psychological adage that anyone who is screaming at you is angry not with you but with himself. It was only after this epiphany that we began to have the peace of mind to work out what way to shove the tiller when the luff bulges back.

'The French have long known that bellowing and psychotherapy are not essential to the student sailor. The Centre Nautique des Glenans, the island sea school in Brittany where I served a short sentence during my teens, was run in virtual silence, except during the initiation rituals, which were loosely based on Foreign Legion practices and involved new uses for lifejackets. The central philosophy appeared to my 15-year-old mind to be 'learn to sail or die.' Our instructor had a speech impediment caused by the Gauloise worn in his mouth. He would point at a distant rock intermittently visible between bursts of spray. "Okay, scum," he would say in French, a language I had learned at high speed, also to survive. "Today you sail round zat rock."

'"Easy!" I would cry happily. "It cannot be more than five miles!"

'"Not so fast, rosbif," snarled the instructor. "Today, you do eet wiz no ruddair."

'And off we went, into the jaws of death. And learned a lot about how to balance jib against main against centreboard, in the tense silence of complete concentration.'

'Yeah, well, fascinating,' said Frank, who does not hold with foreigners. 'Look out!'

We dumped the jib and spilled wind from the main. The dinghy containing the crew of the yacht with the broken mast came alongside. We helped her aboard and gave her a glass of wine. 'Now,' I said, 'we will sail.'

'Never again,' she said, raising her arm as if to ward off a blow.

'Think of it as applied weightlessness,' I said in a sort of murmur.

'Would you mind picking up that red bit of string on your left and pulling it a bit?'

'Like this?'

'Exactly like that.'

The jib filled. *Daisy* started to move. 'This is lovely,' said the woman, swigging deeply at her glass.

Behind us, the man on the mud was howling ambulance and lifeboat. 'Listen to him,' said Frank.

'I fear,' I murmured, 'that experience has taught me never to listen when people shout on boats. A trifle more on the mainsheet, do you think?'

ADRENALINE

A bloke called Arthur has turned up in Mudd Harbour. We were chatting the other day, poodling along in his Drascombe Longboat. 'Will you be crewing for anyone in the Round Mudd Race?' I said, referring to the social event of the early season.

'Crewing?' said Arthur, shocked. 'I'm *entering*.'

'But Drascombes are too light,' I said. 'Notice of Race specifies 1,000kg minimum.'

'That,' said Arthur, 'is why I shall be sailing with two anvils lashed one either side of the centreboard case. My Portsmouth Yardstick is highly beneficial, being somewhere in the early 1300s. I intend to win on corrected time by hard sailing.'

'Oh,' I said, unnerved by this level of gung, or perhaps ho.

Everyone except Arthur said they were not going to take the race seriously. But I noticed my friend Dave scrubbing the bottom of his boat with a broom when he thought no-one was looking. And I noticed Torquil taking delivery of a minibus with smoked glass windows the night before the race.

At 0800 on race morning we were reaching to and fro off the Royal Mudd Yacht Club, breeze SW Force 4, visibility good, HW ten minutes gone. Barry had come along to crew, powerboats like his Baywatch 37 (metres, not feet) being ineligible for the Round Mudd. He was asking if it was normal that the boat was all tipped over like this. The five minute gun had gone, and Dave could be heard shouting at the red-headed girl he had invited to crew in the saloon bar of the Duck and Crumpet the previous evening. The red-headed girl was shouting back. Either they were hove to or something had gone wrong in the middle of a tack.

On the one-minute gun, Torquil's boat shot past with a sound like tearing calico and a bow-wave reaching aft as far as the cockpit. Arranged along the weather rail was a minibusload of small boys, at whom Torquil was yelling in Latin, his khaki shorts flapping like pistol shots. Immediately behind Torquil Arthur came screeching through, trapezing from a bit of string attached to his Drascombe's hounds, the anvils having reduced his freeboard to 1¾ inches.

Torquil crossed the line early and had to come back. Dave fouled someone while involuntarily going astern under sail, and began yelling about rights of way. Arthur made a perfect start at the pin end and hurtled off towards the first mark. 'Jib in, Barry, if you would be so kind,' I said. 'Sorry. I mean, could you pull that bit of string by your right hand? Thanks.' We started.

And off we sailed, halfway up the fleet, or halfway down, depending on how you look at it. The long day wore on.

Having restarted, Torquil rushed round the wrong downwind mark and beat back to go round the right one. Occasionally the sound of clattering canvas and mutual cursing indicated the proximity of Dave. Ahead, Arthur's sails shrank steadily towards the horizon . . .

I picked up the glasses. Not towards the horizon. Towards the surface of the sea. The Drascombe had not shrunk but sunk, and Arthur was sitting in water up to his neck, looking resolute. All around him the fleet sailed grimly on, intent on victory.

Well, we went alongside, and as he caught our line the Drascombe slid smoothly into the deep.

'Tch,' I said, sympathizing over the loss of his boat.

'Yeah, hell,' said Arthur. 'I was well ahead.'

In time the anvils fell out, and the Drascombe bobbed back up, and we bailed her out and Arthur sailed home disqualified. Torquil had mistaken a cardinal for a mark and was halfway to France. Dave had sailed into a wreck and was shouting some more at the redhead, who was shouting some more at Dave.

The sun sank in the west. Along we burbled, chatting of this and that, and eventually crossed the finish line 324th out of 411.

'I enjoyed that,' said Barry. 'Specially the wine.'

'A great British sportsman once said that the reason he took up sailing was that he could not think of any other Olympic sport in which you could light a fag while crossing the start line,' I said. 'Filthy habit, but as a Minimum Racer one sees his point. Goodness, look at the time, the pubs will be shutting, this is serious. Pull that string again.'

By dint of hard sailing we beat closing time by twenty-three minutes, a personal best.

DARKNESS VISIBLE

APOCALYPSE HO

Dave's heat exchanger caved in the other day, so I went out to give him a hand. As the light faded we knocked off and opened a beer. Dave remarked that spring was in the air. He was right. The curlews were yodelling on the flats, and (surest sign of all) Barry's Baywatch 37 (metres, not feet) was on the fuel dock, gassing up for the year's first booze cruise.

'4,300 litres it is,' said Colin the fuel dock.

Barry handed him a wad of fifties and left the dock with a sound like thunder in a dustbin, secure in the knowledge that he was carrying fuel for 300 nautical miles. We watched him draw a four-lane highway of wake over the horizon. 'What is he going to do when the red diesel runs out?' said Dave.

'Pay more money,' I said.

'And when the oil runs out?'

'Learn to row.'

We moved down to the saloon, lit the wood stove, found the whisky and considered the Apocalypse to come. Water flowing down Bond Street. Lifeboats at work on the M4. The South Coast drowned, East Anglia a distant memory. Stick your head in the sea and you hear a thousand church bells, ding dong glug.

'Sounds wonderful,' said Dave.

'Up to a point,' I said. 'Minimum techniques will come into their own. Shore power will be a thing of the past, and so will engines. No longer will marina staff mince to and fro saluting the owners of anything over 30 feet and sneering at the owners of anything smaller. They will stand alertly on the hammerheads, waiting for the heaving line, then joining the sturdy rogues at the capstan bars who will warp us in. We will be inching out of tight slots with poles and lines and little sips of breeze in sails. No boat will go alongside anything without first laying out a hook, in case the wind blows onshore and they need to warp off. Stout wooden tenders will once again come into their own, because they are easy to row into the teeth of a fresh breeze with a hundredweight of anchor sitting in the back end. The youth of the harbour will grow big and strong thanks to the noble labour of umbrella warping – '

'Umbrella what?' said Dave.

'Umbrella warping is the lost art of laying out an anchor, hauling yourself up to it, then laying out another anchor, raising the first, and hauling yourself up to the second, at which point the first is laid out again, and so on. By this means an eighteenth-century ship of the line could travel as much as two cables a day under a plunging fire from shore batteries.'

Dave said that he refused to believe this, and that anyway there are no shore batteries in Mudd Harbour, which in this scenario would also have ceased to exist. I dismissed this as a technicality. 'A world without oil will be a new, cleaner world, and Minimum Boat people will be ready for it,' I said. 'We will kedge in deep water while we wait for the tide to turn fair. There will be no more outboards, merely an oar in the transom-notch of the dinghy. The GPS satellites will be mere streaks of plasma in the night sky. We will use chip logs, sextants, leadlines, copal varnish and Stockholm tar. We will say farewell to onboard stereo, and hey nonny no to unaccompanied folk song.'

Here, as far as I remember, we started singing. When we woke the next day there were empty bottles everywhere, a thin grey rain and no wind. We stared at the heat exchanger with acute dislike. 'Engine'll have to come out,' said Dave. 'We'll go alongside. Shall we wait for a breeze, or do you want to umbrella warp?'

I tried to conceal a strong shudder at the prospect. Just then, distant thunder rumbled beyond the headland. Barry's *Capitalist Tool* slid into view, loaded down to her summer marks with fine beers. I rushed onto the foredeck, waving the end of a bit of anchorplait. Barry slowed, ready to take us in tow. 'You can't,' said Dave.

'We can,' I said.

And we did.

MINIMUM CRANEAGE

Well the winter is upon us, the skies are full of geese, and Dick the Shepherd blows his nail (Shakespeare). Not that I care. For it is time to get *Daisy* into the shed for the annual operations.

Or so I was saying to my friend Dave, him that owns the beautiful long-keel sloop that is too big to sail singlehanded, take anywhere interesting or (as it turns out) sell. We were sort of huddled over Dave's Eberspacher in Mudd Harbour. 'Me too,' he said. 'I have got to get the boat craned out. I have got to get the sails valeted and the diesel inhibited and some scratches unscratched. The radar and the wind instruments are mostly aluminium oxide and the anchor chain needs replacing and the anode has gone invisible so I shudder to think what state the skin fittings are in. It is going to cost thousands. I hate it,' said Dave. 'As soon as those crane slings go under the boat we are at the mercy of the shark pack. Is that whisky in the bottle?'

'Lamp oil, I think.'

He drank it anyway. 'You're right,' he said, taking another swig. 'But we must not repine. This is the way it is.'

I said. 'It need not be thus.'

'Wha?'

'Allow me to explain Minimum Craneage,' I said. 'As you know, my boat has a trailer. But in some circumstances a trailer can be an admission of failure.'

'Poetic,' said Dave.

'A mere morceau,' I said, returning to my theme with an airy wave. 'Rather than undergo a version of the clammy process you describe, I shall be sailing my boat up various rivers to a yard mostly full of narrowboats which is just round the corner from where I live. There I will stick her on the trailer and haul her back to the barn for the winter work.'

'If I tried to go up a river, I'd go aground after mile three,' said Dave.

'Very true.' I spoke distractedly. I had indeed meant to trail *Daisy* home from Mudd. But as the lamp oil flowed, I began to fill in the details of my scheme. And after I had rowed back to the boat later, I started poring over various almanacs and charts, plus the canal and river Stoppage Programme. I passed a sleepless but comfortable night. The following morning, I made calls to everyone I knew saying I had a touch of flu but would probably be better in a month. And off I set.

Of the actual Minimum Craneage voyage, which covered plenty of coast, even more river and a certain amount of canal, I shall not speak at this point. What did emerge were a few rules of conduct for the Minimum Boat on a journey through falling leaves into the dark of winter. I print them below in the hope that they may help.

1. Beware of Brown Floods. A river in autumn spate flows at about five knots, and *Daisy* motors at about five and a quarter. Under such circumstances it is possible to ferry-glide from Windsor to Eton and back again almost indefinitely.

2. Measure your mast. Bridges are usually higher than they look. But not always. Particularly not during Brown Floods (see above) near Maidenhead.

3. Beware of all Home Counties. As a west countryman, I automatically assume that those little notices by the canal say things like NEW LAID EGGS VERY CHEAP and WELCOME, STRANGER. In the Home Counties they are more likely to say YOU ARE COMMITTING AN ACT OF CRIMINAL TRESPASS ON CCTV.

4. Beware of the Towpath Dog. Obviously.

5. Handling Ice. Ice forms on rivers when they get cold, particularly in lock cuts. Two inches of ice is not safe to stand on, so you may think

it is quite weak. But when you are trying to motor a small boat down a 50ft lock cut covered in two-inch ice you will find it resists your progress. This is because the ice you are trying to penetrate is actually fifty feet thick, end on. At this point it becomes clear why most icebreakers are nuclear. Fresh out of plutonium? Break it up with an oar. Buy a new propeller later.

6. Cabin heat. Cabins get very very cold, particularly on the Sharpness Canal. Narrow boats have wood stoves, fuelled by driftwood. *Daisy*'s cabin is big enough for a wood stove, but not at the same time as a person. Coleman lamps, the gas model, give heat as well as light.

7. Christmas comes but once a year. And that goes for Boxing Day too. Christmas is a day for putting the mast back up, dressing over all with fairy lights, and hoisting a tree to the maintruck. Boxing Day is a day for dropping the mast on your toe, forgetting which way the river is flowing, and accepting seasonal drinks from a harbourmaster at a port near the limit of navigation on the Severn.

8. The day after Boxing Day is for having a headache and discovering that the crane charge is £25 per metre plus ice surcharge, attempting to do it with slipway and trailer during a brown flood (see above), getting hypothermic, cursing all the way home, slamming the barn doors on the boat and swearing you are never going near the damn thing ever again.

9. The day before New Year's Eve is for saying the hell with it, we always sail on New Year's Day and always will, towing the boat down to Mudd Harbour and having a dynamite sail in a harbour empty except for Dave, who has had a cashflow crisis and moved to a swinging mooring seven miles from the nearest quay.

10. The New Year segues into gales from the northwest and heavy rain. It is time to stop messing about, lay up and start on the refit with the knowledge that while Minimum Craneage may not be quicker or cheaper than the conventional model, on the whole it is better than watching the telly.

BOAT SHOW

There are an awful lot of Boat Shows about nowadays. In the Dugong and Octopus the other night we agreed that our feet were sore from tramping the stands and the strain was getting just about intolerable. So why, said Dave, do we not stay at home and put on a Minimum Boat Show right here in Mudd? Anyone want a drink?

What a very interesting idea, we all said gravely. Put your card behind the bar and explain. Take your time.

So he did. And we instantly formed a Steering Committee, secured liability insurance, and got on to the vital question of sponsorship. Dave suggested Swiss Tony's Boat Brokers, motto, selling a boat is like making love to a beautiful woman who smells of diesel and bilge. Bert explained that brokers were not to be trusted. We compromised on the WI. After all, really excellent tea and cakes are the foundation of a good Boat Show.

So here is the draft prospectus for the Mudd Minimum Boat Show. Obviously there will be boats. Three, actually. They will be sited in the glamorous car park at the Mudd Lidl. There will be *Daisy* in a cradle with her sails up. There will be Dave's boat in another cradle with her sails up. And there will be Hex's *Ronette*, lying around on the tarmac with her sails up. If there is any wind at all they will all blow over, but worse things happen at sea. The idea is that visitors to the show will come in, buy a cake and perhaps a cup of tea, and stroll around the boats peering into the cabins from stepladders and thinking: I wouldn't half mind one of them, there would be plenty of room in there if someone did the washing up.

But of course we realise that not everyone goes to a Boat Show to buy a boat. Many people have boats of their own for which they require gadgets. At the MBS these will be simple and effective. There will be the Hubbogrill, a dedicated inboard-outboard barbecue facility made out of an old Mini wheel and some weldmesh. There will be the Acme Stabbo Harpoon (Say Goodbye to Vast Eel Misery) made from size 01 conger hooks straightened out and glued to a bamboo. And there will be the Apollo 13 Mastclimb System (£2,750). Just attach special dedicated water containers (provided) to main halyard and hoist to top of mast. Then fill with water using hosepipe, climb into bosun's chair at other end of halyard and cut thin string anchoring bosun's chair to deck with dedicated Stanley knife (provided). Enjoy air whooshing past face. And there you are among the gulls (not provided). How you get down is still subject to development work. The state of the art is to call the coastguard who will alert SAR helicopters.

Naturally there will also be demonstrations. Market research found a big following for the Egg Frying, consisting as it does of converting raw eggs to fried eggs under simulated marine conditions (stove on end of seesaw). The Man Overboard simulator was good until the fatality. And the Blocked Head Simulator was justly unpopular.

But actually what everyone wants at a Boat Show is Corporate Hospitality and Cheap Stuff. Corporate Hospitality will be provided by the WI with the able assistance of Doris Strong, in which Doris, five times winner of the Surfers against Sewage Wet T-shirt competition (Lizard Branch) demonstrates the use of the solar shower. And there will be a lot of cheap stuff, such as old saucepans and bits of string, and a licensed bar to overcome consumer resistance.

Naturally the whole thing will make a cracking loss, but this is normal with boat shows. To fix this it has been resolved that next year we are going to sell the concept for big money to a mad suit who will double the floor space and arrange a personal appearance by Britney Spears. That should do the trick, the way it has at Southampton, Earl's Court, ExCeL, Timbuktu and Ulan Bator. Naturally we will be long gone by then. Meanwhile, watch this space and see you there!

MINIMUM MINIMUM

The poet Robert Service once observed that there are many strange things done under the midnight sun. If he had been around in the far northwest of Scotland the other summer, he would have wagged his head and said 'I told you so.'

A few of us Minimum Boats were anchored in a sea loch north of Ardnamurchan. Outside the entrance, a Force 6 breeze was picking up large grey lumps of sea and depositing them on other lumps of sea, causing alarm and despondency to nearby sailormen. Inside the loch, the breeze was combed to a murmur by the Caledonian pine forest, and we were drinking a spot of wine and speaking of this and that. When suddenly out of the grim murk to seaward there appeared a selection of sails.

At first I thought they were big boats far away. Then I realised that they were small boats close at hand. And in they came, one after another, streaking out of the rough and into the smooth. They nosed into the glassy shallows under the reflections of the pines. They came head to wind in line abreast. There were two men to each boat, dressed in wetsuits. One man dropped an anchor. The other man dropped the sails. Then, synchronising their movements for balance, each duo sat down one on either side of the centreboard case, facing aft.

Steam rose from kettles. The outside arm of each man appeared, bearing a mug of tea, rested it on the gunwale for a moment, and raised mug to lips. The operation was perfectly synchronised. It had to be, or the dinghies would have rocked and the hardy inmates would have got lapfuls of boiling water. The operation proceeded with simultaneous sipping, synchronised aah-that's-bettering, and temporally integrated dreg-emptying.

Tea done and cups simultaneously rinsed, the dinghy cruisers put up tents. All movements were neat, precise and robotic. There is a kind of tent used by climbers known as the Don Whillans Box, assembled with extreme care because it is designed to hang from a piton over thousand-foot cliffs. The care and precision used by the dinghists was in the Don Whillans category.

I am a nosy person. After a while I could stand it no longer. I slid alongside one of the boats. 'Hello,' I said.

A flap unzipped. A neat head emerged. 'Hello,' said the head.

'Where have you come from?'

'Loch Scavaig,' he said.

'God almighty,' I said. Scavaig is a beauteous but savage notch in Skye. To get here from there, this frail cockleshell and its chums would have had to brave Point of Sleat and the tide-whipped skerries off Arisaig, all in breezes of Force 5 and above.

'We have a good pump,' said the head.

'And self-bailers,' said an invisible voice from inside the tent.

'Great planing,' said the head.

'*Fast* planing,' said Invisible. 'You don't plane, do you?'

'Too heavy,' said the head. I was getting the impression that everything about this dinghy was balanced, even the speech patterns of its occupants.

'Plane?' I said, with a light shudder and a slap on *Daisy*'s meaty side. 'I should jolly well think not. Forgive my asking, but what are you cooking?'

'Extreme Noodles, dried,' said Invisible.

'Survival Stew, dehydrated,' said Head.

'Fancy a glass of whisky, wet?' I said.

There was a short, perfectly-balanced silence. Then two mugs appeared. I sloshed stuff into them. One of them was shaking. 'Cold?' I said.

'No,' said Head.

'Bit,' said Invisible.

'Come aboard,' I said.

They were wearing thermal underwear, and (in Invisible's case) goose pimples the size of his Adam's apple. I made tea, put a bit more whisky in it, and gave Invisible a sleeping bag to put over himself. He looked around *Daisy*'s infinitesimal cabin with the expression of a mole suddenly finding itself in the Albert Hall. 'It's huge,' he said, awed.

'It's the Minimum Boat,' I said.

He nodded insincerely. He was warming up, and a weird light was coming to his eye. 'Built-in stove,' he said. 'Two bunks. Plus a cockpit with somewhere to sit. And built-in ballast so if you get knocked down you come up again.'

'And very nice too,' I said.

'If you want to wallow in unnecessary luxury,' he said.

'Wallow?' I said, shocked.

'In a boat that doesn't plane, wallow is what you do.'

'Excuse me – '

'This is not a Minimum Boat,' he said. 'It is a floating Grand Hotel. Oil lamp, forsooth! Bookshelf, tchah!' He sloshed more of my whisky into his tea, huddled into the sleeping bag and rolled his eyes up to the deckhead of *Daisy*'s nice comfortable cabin, curling his blasted lip. I considered throwing him overboard. But part of Minimum Boating is never to do anything that will eventually do itself. So I said, 'Well, one man's minimum is another man's Grand Hotel, and vice versa, I suppose. Meanwhile the nights are drawing in, and I have a couscous to cook. I expect your Extreme Noodles will be fully hydrated by now. Wouldn't want them to get soggy, eh?'

'No,' he said, and they left; casting, I have to say, a look of regret at *Daisy*'s hospitable interior as they wriggled symmetrically into the clammy recesses of their tent.

Well, the couscous was very good, and I saw the dinghists casting balanced glances of an envious nature through the chemical steam of their Survival Stew. Next morning off they set. And I have to say that as their little boats lifted onto the plane and streaked for the horizon, I did see their point. Head waved, and I waved back. Then I heard Invisible sneeze. The poor man seemed to have caught a cold. Another cup of coffee would bring us to low water, I thought. Then perhaps northward, for Kyle Rea.

MINIMUM MINIMUM MINIMUM

The boat is on the trailer in the barn awaiting a refit, and everyone is thrashing about looking for something to do. Or certainly Barry was when I saw him the other night. He was en route to a crisis meeting with his bankers. There were soup stains on his blazer. I pointed them out.

'Soup?' he said. 'No way, mate. Epoxy.'

I was shocked. Barry is the owner of a Baywatch 37 (metres, not feet). 'Epoxy?' I cried. 'What is someone like you doing messing around with that fearsome and unconquerable goo?'

'Building a boat, innit,' said Barry.

I shook my head. Hearing that a Baywatch proprietor is building his own boat is like hearing that HM the Queen is polishing her own crown.

'My daughter's baby is due next month,' said Barry. 'I am making a stitch-and-glue 3ft pram dinghy that will serve first as a cradle and then as a garden pond runabout for the new life within. The build programme takes place in odd moments like on the way here when I had already changed for the meeting. But I put in too much hardener and got stuck to the boat and the wife had to cut me loose. Grandchildren, eh? It will be a lovely little thing.'

'Grandchildren are,' I said.

'Grandchildren are only babies,' said Barry. 'I am referring to the boat.'

At some point in the foregoing, Torquil had arrived on the other side of the table, where he was scowling heavily over the rim of a glass of red wine. 'Epoxy?' he said. 'Tchah.'

'What's wrong with it?'

'It is derived from oil,' said Torquil. 'It is highly toxic, allergenic, goes straight to the liver and persists in the environment for centuries. Furthermore it is too easy. Personally I am building a 14ft clinker dinghy along lines suggested by the immortal John Leather, to whose book on Clinker Boatbuilding I owe everything. We have made meticulous preparations and many of our own tools. We have felled the trees, dried the timber, built the mould, cut the planks, clamped what needs clamping, built a 17-part stem assembly using boiled glue, prepared copper nails and rooves, and are ready to commence.'

'You and whose army are doing this?' said Barry, rather coarsely.

Torquil drew himself up to his full glass. 'I am lucky to have the assistance of form 4b, who are contributing to the project in exchange for bonus marks in their Latin SATs.' We nodded. Torquil treats his pupils as if he were Captain Bligh and they were a bunch of Lascar foc'sle hands. 'Besides, the boat is a thing of pure classical simplicity, larch on elm, wineglass transom, and of course three ringbolts for hoisting it on deck via the spare halyard.'

'With six ten-year-olds on the other end.'

'Winches are technology gone mad. Besides, the boys love it. Dave, what's that stuff on your hands?'

'Glue,' said Dave, who is becoming frugal to the point of miserliness. 'Coincidentally, I am boatbuilding myself. I found this old Avon Redstart in a skip and it has only got fourteen holes in it plus some thin spots, so I am doing a full restoration with hypalon glue and bits of old wetsuit. My old tender is knackered.'

There was a pause as we all tried to imagine a tender more knackered than the one he had just described. 'And you,' he said, turning to me. 'Building a Minimum Boat, is it?'

'Thinking about it,' I said.

This was a lie. I have just built a boat, and I am pretty sure it is the Minimum. It is based on something I saw fishing off Yap, a swampy bump in the Pacific some 750 nautical miles east of the Philippines. To build, take two 8ft x 4ft sheets of used corrugated iron. Bend first sheet double along long axis. Sew up ends with fence wire. Force apart the centre and insert a bit of wood lengthways, to keep the sides apart. You now have a basic canoe form. Repeat, using the other sheet of corrugated iron. You now have two basic canoe forms. Caulk all holes with 3:1 mix of sand and cement. Using two stout bamboos or other timbers, lash canoes side by side in a catamaran configuration. Allow cement to set. Launch. Fish, bailing for your life.

'Complicated business, boatbuilding,' said Torquil.

I nodded, of course. But what I actually meant was, for the true Minimum boatman, nothing is ever complicated. Because if it is, it is not properly Minimum.

PEYTON